Easy Steps to Chinese

3 TEXTBOOK

轻松学中文

SIMPLIFIED
CHARACTERS
VERSION

Yamin Ma
Xinying Li

北京语言大学出版社
BEIJING LANGUAGE AND CULTURE
UNIVERSITY PRESS

图书在版编目（CIP）数据

轻松学中文.课本.第3册：马亚敏，李欣颖编著
－北京：北京语言大学出版社，2013 重印
ISBN 978-7-5619-1889-0

Ⅰ.轻... Ⅱ.①马...②李... Ⅲ.汉语－对外汉语教学
－教材 Ⅳ.H195.4

中国版本图书馆 CIP 数据核字(2007)第 096544 号

书　　名	**轻松学中文**.课本.第 3 册
责任编辑	苗　强　王亚莉
美术策划	王　宇
封面设计	王　宇　王章定
版式设计	王章定
责任印制	汪学发

出版发行　北京语言大学出版社
社　　址　北京市海淀区学院路 15 号　邮政编码：100083
网　　址　www.blcup.com

电　　话　编辑部 010-8230 3647
　　　　　发行部 010-8230 3650/3591/3651/3080
　　　　　读者服务部 010-8230 3653/3908
网上订购　010-8230 3668　service@blcup.com
印　　刷　北京联兴盛业印刷股份有限公司
经　　销　全国新华书店

版　　次　2007 年 7 月第 1 版　2013 年 5 月第 8 次印刷
开　　本　889 毫米×1194 毫米　1/16　印张：10.75
字　　数　134 千字
书　　号　ISBN 978-7-5619-1889-0/H.07109
　　　　　11800

Easy Steps to Chinese *(Textbook 3)*
Yamin Ma, Xinying Li

Editor	Qiang Miao, Yali Wang
Art design	Arthur Y. Wang
Cover design	Arthur Y. Wang, Zhangding Wang
Graphic design	Zhangding Wang

Published by
Beijing Language & Culture University Press
No.15 Xueyuan Road, Haidian District, Beijing, China 100083

Distributed by
Beijing Language & Culture University Press
No.15 Xueyuan Road, Haidian District, Beijing, China 100083

First published in July 2007

Website: www.blcup.com

ACKNOWLEDGEMENTS

A number of people have helped us to put the books into publication. Particular thanks are owed to the following:

- 戚德祥先生、张健女士 who trusted our expertise in the field of Chinese language teaching and learning

- Editors 苗强先生、王亚莉女士 for their meticulous work

- Graphic designers 娄禹先生、王章定先生 for their artistic design

- Art consultant Arthur Y. Wang and artists 陆颖、顾海燕、龚华伟、王净 for their artistic ability in the illustrations

- Edward Qiu who assisted the authors with the sound recording

- And finally, members of our families who have always given us generous support.

INTRODUCTION

- Easy Steps to Chinese includes 8 books and has three stages: Stage 1–Books 1 and 2; Stage 2–Books 3, 4, 5 and 6; and Stage 3–Books 7 and 8. The primary goal of this series *Easy Steps to Chinese* is to help the students establish a solid foundation of vocabulary, knowledge of Chinese and communication skills through the natural and gradual integration of language, content and cultural elements. This series adopts a holistic approach, and is designed to emphasize the development of communication skills in listening, speaking, reading and writing.

- *Easy Steps to Chinese* comprises 8 colour textbooks, each of them supplemented by a CD, a workbook (starting from Book 6, the textbook and workbook are combined into one book), a teacher's book with a CD and unit tests. Books 1-3 are also accompanied by picture flashcards, word cards and posters.

COURSE DESIGN

The design of this series has achieved:

- **A balance between authentic and modified language**
  All the oral and written materials have been modified and carefully selected to suit the students' level, so that a gradual development of the target language can be achieved.

- **A balance of focus on language and culture**
  This series provides ample opportunities for the students to experience the language and its culture in order to develop intercultural awareness and enrich their personal experience.

- **A balance between language knowledge and communication skills**
  Explicit knowledge of the target language is necessary and important for the students to achieve accuracy, fluency and overall communication skills. This series is designed to ensure that knowledge-based language learning is placed within a communicative context, resulting in the improvement of both linguistic knowledge and performance.

- **A balance between a broad and controlled course**
  This series serves as a core while offering a broad range of vocabulary, topics and various text types to meet the different needs of the students.

简介

- 《轻松学中文》共八册，分为三个阶段。第一阶段为第一、二册；第二阶段为第三、四、五、六册；第三阶段为第七、八册。此套教材旨在帮助汉语为非母语的中、小学生奠定扎实的汉语学习基础。此目标是通过语言、话题和文化的自然结合，从词汇、汉语知识的学习及语言交流技能的培养两个方面来达到的。此套教材把汉语作为一个整体来教授，在教学过程中十分注重听、说、读、写四项交际技能的培养。

- 《轻松学中文》每册包括一本彩色课本（附一张CD），一本练习册（第六、七、八册课本与练习册合成一册），一本教师用书(附单元测验试卷及一张CD)，1–3册还配有词语卡片、图卡和教学挂图。

课程设计

本套教材的课程设计力图达到：

- 地道语言与调整语言的平衡
  为了使学生的汉语程度能循序渐进地提高，本套教材中的口语及书面语都经过严谨的选择，并作过适当的调整。

- 语言与文化的平衡
  为了培养学生的多元文化意识，丰富他们的经历，本套教材为学生接触汉语及中国文化提供了各种各样的机会。

- 语言知识与交际能力的平衡
  为了能在听、说、读、写四项技能方面准确并流利地运用汉语，学生对语言知识的掌握不仅是重要的，而且也是必要的。本套教材把语言知识的学习与语言技能的培养巧妙地结合在一起，力求使学生在增加汉语知识的同时提高运用语言的能力。

- 扩展与控制的平衡
  本套教材不仅可以作为汉语教学的"主

- **A balance between the "oral speech" and the "written form"**
  This series aims to balance the importance of both oral and written communication skills. The development of writing skills is embedded in the course, while oral communication skills are being developed from the outset.

This series covers:

- Pinyin is introduced to the students from the very beginning. The pinyin above the Chinese characters is gradually removed to ensure a smooth transition.

- Chinese characters are taught according to the character formation system. Once the students have a good grasp of radicals and simple characters, they will be able to analyze most of the compound characters they encounter, and to memorize new characters in a logical way.

- Grammar and sentence structures are explained in note form. The students are expected to use correct grammar and compound sentence structures in both oral and written forms to communicate when their overall level of Chinese has steadily improved over the years.

- Dictionary skills are taught once they have learned radicals and simple characters. The students are encouraged to use dictionaries whenever appropriate in order to become independent learners.

- Typing skills are taught when the students have learned some basic knowledge of Chinese.

- Listening practice is designed to help the students develop their ability to infer meanings of unfamiliar words and content.

- Speaking practice involves students using Chinese to communicate their thoughts spontaneously in real-life situations with accuracy and fluency.

- Reading skills are developed through regular reading of simple passages to suit the students' level. Gradually, they will develop skills and confidence when reading articles in newspapers, magazines or on the Internet in order to expand their vocabulary and knowledge of modern China, and to get in touch with the current issues emerging within China and around the world.

- Writing skills are gradually developed through a process of guided writing on topics familiar to the students. Written tasks will become easier, as the students learn to organize their thoughts coherently and logically, and develop the skills to select appropriate vocabulary, sentence structures and genres to construct an effective written piece with accuracy and fluency.

线"，而且所提供的大量词汇、话题及各式各样的文体还可满足不同水平学生的需要。

- "语"与"文"的平衡
  本套教材力图使学生在口语及书面语两个方面同时提高。写作能力及口头交际能力的培养贯穿始终。

本套教材所包括的内容有：

- 拼音是初级阶段教学重点之一。附在汉字上面的拼音将逐渐取消以确保平稳过渡。

- 汉字是根据汉字的结构来教授的。学生一旦掌握了一定数量的偏旁部首和独体字，他们就有能力分析遇到的大部分合体字，并能有条理地记忆生字。

- 语法及句型是以注解的方式来解释的。经过几年有条不紊的学习，学生可望在口头及书面交流时运用正确的语法及复合句型。

- 查字典、词典的技能是在学生学会了部分偏旁部首及独体字后才开始培养的。为了培养学生的独立学习能力，教师要经常鼓励学生自己查字典、词典来完成某项功课。

- 打字技能的培养是在学生已经掌握了一些汉语基本知识后才开始的。

- 听力练习力图培养学生猜生字的意思及文章内容的能力。

- 口语练习设计旨在培养学生用准确、流利的汉语在现实生活中跟人即兴沟通、交流。

- 阅读练习旨在鼓励学生养成每天阅读简短篇章的习惯，从而帮助学生提高阅读能力，树立阅读信心。高年级阶段，学生可望读懂报纸、杂志及因特网上的简短文章，以便扩大词汇量，增加对现代中国的了解。

- 写作能力的培养需要一个长期的过程。学生先在教师的指导下写他们所熟悉的话题，直到能够运用适当的词汇、语句、体裁，有条理地、准确地、恰当地、有效地交流思想。

The focus of each stage:

- Stage 1 (Books 1 and 2): ◆ pinyin ◆ strokes and stroke order ◆ the structures of Chinese characters ◆ tracing of characters ◆ radicals and simple characters ◆ dictionary skills ◆ typing skills ◆ listening skills ◆ speaking skills ◆ reading skills ◆ writing skills: guided written assignments around 100 characters

- Stage 2 (Books 3, 4, 5 and 6): ◆ radicals and simple characters ◆ formation of phrases ◆ expansion of vocabulary ◆ simple grammar and sentence structures ◆ dictionary skills ◆ typing skills ◆ classroom instruction in Chinese ◆ listening skills ◆ speaking skills ◆ reading skills ◆ writing skills: guided written assignments between 100-300 characters ◆ exposure to modern China and Chinese culture

- Stage 3 (Books 7 and 8): ◆ classroom instruction in Chinese ◆ expansion of vocabulary ◆ grammar and sentence structures ◆ dictionary skills ◆ typing skills ◆ listening and speaking skills through spontaneous interaction ◆ reading practice on a daily basis ◆ writing skills: independent written assignments between 300-500 characters ◆ exposure to modern China and its culture ◆ contemporary topics: current issues around the world

COURSE LENGTH

- This series is designed for non-Chinese background students at both primary and secondary levels. Book 1 starts with basic knowledge of Chinese. Students at primary 5 or 6, or Year 7 students at secondary level can start with Book 1.

- With three periods, of approximately three hours per week, most students will be able to complete one book within one academic year. Fast learners can spend less than a year completing one book. As the 8 books of this series are continuous and ongoing, each book can be taught within any time span.

每个阶段的教学重点：

- 第一阶段（第一、二册）：◆ 拼音 ◆ 笔画和笔顺 ◆字形结构 ◆ 描红 ◆ 偏旁部首和独体字 ◆ 查字典 ◆ 打字 ◆ 听力 ◆ 口语 ◆ 阅读 ◆写作（100个字左右）

- 第二阶段（第三、四、五、六册）：◆偏旁部首和独体字 ◆词语构成 ◆词汇扩展 ◆语法及句型结构 ◆查字典、词典 ◆打字 ◆课堂用语 ◆听力 ◆口语 ◆阅读 ◆写作（100-300字）◆接触现代中国和中国文化

- 第三阶段（第七、八册）：◆课堂用语 ◆词汇扩展 ◆语法及句型结构 ◆查字典、词典 ◆打字 ◆听力 ◆口语 ◆阅读 ◆独立写作（300-500字）◆时事

课程进度

- 本套教材为非华裔中、小学生编写。因为第一册从最基本的汉语知识教起，所以学生不需要有任何汉语知识背景。学生可以从小学五、六年级开始使用第一册，也可以从中学一年级开始使用第一册。

- 如果每星期上三节课，每节课在一小时左右，大部分学生可在一年之内学完一册。如果有些学生学得比较快，他们可以加快进度，不到一年就学完一册书。由于本套教材是连贯的，老师可以在任何时段内根据学生的水平来决定教学进度。

HOW TO USE THIS BOOK

Here are a few suggestions as to how to use this book:

The teacher should:

- first let the students read aloud the phonetic exercises in the textbook, then correct inaccurate pronunciation as appropriate.

- advise the students to read through the questions before listening to the recording when doing listening comprehension exercises.

- emphasize the importance of radicals and simple characters. Students should try to memorize all radicals and simple characters previously introduced in order to assist their learning of compound characters.

- review vocabulary, grammar and sentence structures introduced in the previous books and encourage students to use them accurately, appropriately and functionally in both oral speech and written work.

- make flexible use of the activities in the textbook, which are designed to help students master vocabulary, use of grammar and sentence structures.

- create opportunities for the students to practise their dictionary and typing skills.

- provide every opportunity for students to develop their listening and speaking skills during class time. A variety of authentic situations for the functional use of Chinese created in the textbook can be modified according to the students' ability.

- modify, extend or omit exercises according to the students' levels. A wide variety of exercises in both textbook and workbook can be used for class or homework.

The texts and listening comprehension exercises are on the CD attached to the textbook. The symbol indicates the track number, for example, ◗╍ is track one.

Yamin Ma
July 2007, Hong Kong

怎样使用本册教材

以下是使用本册教材的一些教学建议，仅供教师参考。建议教师：

- 先让学生自己朗读课本里的语音练习。如果学生发音不准，教师可在适当的时候纠正他们的发音。

- 在做听力练习之前，先让学生看问题，然后再听录音。

- 注重偏旁部首和独体字的掌握。教师应该要求学生记住以前学过的偏旁部首和独体字，这样学生日后学合体字会觉得容易得多。

- 经常复习那些在前几册书中出现过的词汇、语法和句型。无论在口语还是书面语中，教师应该要求学生尽量用准确、恰当的词语、语法和句型来有效地与人沟通。

- 灵活地选用课本里的练习。这些练习的设计旨在帮助学生掌握词汇、语法和句型。

- 创造实践机会，提高学生查字典及打字的技能。

- 在课堂上尽量创造机会培养并提高学生的听、说能力。课本里不同类型、贴近现实生活的口语练习情景，可以根据学生的汉语水平作适当的调整。

- 根据学生的能力及水平挑选、修改或扩展某些练习。课本及练习册里的练习可以在课堂上做，也可以让学生带回家做。

每一课的课文、听力练习的录音都附在ＣＤ里。课本录音部分均附有标记和轨迹编号，例如，◗╍ 表示轨迹1。

马亚敏
2007 年 7 月于香港

CONTENTS 目录

Unit 1

Text 1

wǒ men jiā qīn qi bù duō
我们家亲戚不多。
wǒ bà ba jiā de qīn qi
我爸爸家的亲戚
dōu zhù zài měi guó
都住在美国。

wǒ yé ye hé nǎi nai zhù
我爷爷和奶奶住
zài luò shān jī   wǒ dà
在洛杉矶。我大
bó gēn wǒ yé ye hé nǎi
伯跟我爷爷和奶
nai yì qǐ zhù
奶一起住。

wǒ yǒu yí ge shū shu hé
我有一个叔叔和
yí ge gū gu   tā men
一个姑姑。他们
dōu zhù zài niǔ yuē
都住在纽约。

měi nián de shèng dàn jié   wǒ men dōu zài yé ye   nǎi nai jiā guò
每年的圣诞节，我们都在爷爷、奶奶家过。

1

NEW WORDS

1. qīn 亲(親) parent; relative
2. qī 戚 relative
   qīn qi 亲戚 relative
3. yé 爷(爺) grandfather (paternal)
   yé ye 爷爷 grandfather (paternal)
4. nǎi nai 奶奶 grandmother (paternal)
5. luò shān jī 洛杉矶 Los Angeles

6. bó 伯 father's elder brother
   dà bó 大伯 father's elder brother
7. shū 叔 father's younger brother
   shū shu 叔叔 father's younger brother
8. gū 姑 father's sister
   gū gu 姑姑 father's sister
9. niǔ yuē 纽约(紐約) New York

10. měi nián 每年 every year
11. shèng 圣(聖) holy
12. dàn 诞(誕) birth
    shèng dàn jié 圣诞节 Christmas
*13. guò 过(過) spend (time)

• • • 1 •

1 Speaking practice.

Example:

　我家有五口人：爷爷、奶奶，爸爸、妈妈和我。我爷爷和奶奶跟我们一起住。我没有兄弟姐妹。我是独生女。

It is your turn!

Introduce your family.

2 Say the following in Chinese.

爷爷　奶奶

外公　外婆

 姑姑
 伯伯
 爸爸
 妈妈
 舅舅
 姨妈

 弟弟
 哥哥
 我
 姐姐
 妹妹

Extra Words

wài gōng	wài pó	jiù jiu	yí mā
a) 外公	b) 外婆	c) 舅舅	d) 姨妈

3 Read aloud.

1 bàba   2 māma   3 jiějie

4 gēge   5 yéye   6 nǎinai

7 bóbo   8 shūshu   9 jiùjiu

Practice Focus

Neutral Tone

3

4 Translate from Chinese to English.

1. 我在北京住过。

2. 我吃过这种水果。

3. 我看过这个电影。

4. 爸爸也学过法语。

5. 我们家用过这种烤箱。

6. 妈妈在这家医院工作过。

7. 他没有喝过这种饮料。

8. 爸爸跟我一起学汉语。

9. 我喜欢跟哥哥一起打球。

10. 他明年跟姐姐一起住。

11. 我想跟叔叔一起去北京。

12. 妹妹喜欢跟她的朋友一起做作业。

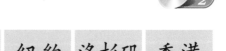

It is your turn!

Make a sentence with "过" and "跟……一起……" respectively.

5 Listen and tick the right boxes.

	北京	上海	伦敦	巴黎	纽约	洛杉矶	香港
小明一家			✓				
大伯							
二伯							
爷爷、奶奶							
姑姑							
叔叔							

6 Make a dialogue with your partner.

《 Sample questions:

1. 你家有几口人？你家有谁？

2. 你爸爸、妈妈都工作吗？他们做什么工作？

3. 你们家亲戚多吗？你爸爸那边有什么亲戚？

4. 你爷爷、奶奶还在吗？他们多大岁数了？

5. 你爷爷、奶奶现在住在哪儿？他们还工作吗？

6. 你每年的圣诞节都在哪儿过？

7. 你今年的圣诞节想去哪儿玩儿？

7 Speaking practice.

Example

我叫钱乐乐。我在上海出生，但是我在加拿大长大。我是加拿大人。我爷爷、奶奶现在住在多伦多。我们一家人现在住在香港。我去过纽约、巴黎和东京……

It is your turn! ➤
Introduce yourself.

5

nǐ wài gōng wài pó zhù zài nǎr
你外公、外婆住在哪儿？

wǒ wài gōng qián nián qù shì le
我外公前年去世了。

wǒ wài pó zhù zài shàng hǎi
我外婆住在上海。

nǐ yǒu ā yí jiù jiu ma
你有阿姨、舅舅吗？

yǒu yí ge yí mā hé yí ge jiù jiu
有一个姨妈和一个舅舅。

tā men yǒu hái zi ma
他们有孩子吗？

yí mā yǒu yí ge nǚ ér
姨妈有一个女儿，

jiù jiu yǒu yí ge ér zi
舅舅有一个儿子。

nǐ cháng gēn wài pó jiàn miàn ma
你常跟外婆见面吗？

cháng jiàn miàn wǒ men měi nián chūn jié
常见面。我们每年春节

dōu gēn wài pó yì qǐ guò
都跟外婆一起过。

1. 外公 wài gōng grandfather (maternal)
2. 婆 pó old woman
   外婆 wài pó grandmother (maternal)
3. 前年 qián nián the year before last
4. 世 shì lifetime
   去世 qù shì pass away

5. 阿 ā prefix
6. 姨 yí mother's sister
   阿姨 ā yí mother's sister
   姨妈 yí mā (married) mother's sister
7. 舅 jiù mother's brother
   舅舅 jiù jiu mother's brother

8. 孩 hái child
   孩子 hái zi child
9. 女儿 nǚ ér daughter
10. 儿子 ér zi son
11. 见面 jiàn miàn meet; see
12. 春节 chūn jié Spring Festival; Chinese New Year

---

8 Fill in the blanks according to the patterns. Give the meanings.

前天		今天 today		后天
		今年		

上个星期	这个星期	
	这个月	

It is your turn!

Choose two words from above and make a sentence with each of them.

---

9 Memorize the following radicals within 3 minutes.

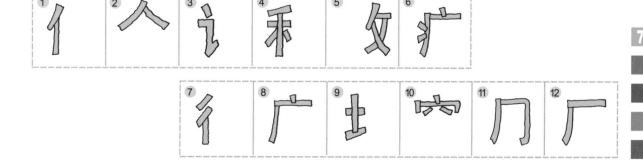

7

10 Ask your partner the following questions.

1. 你们家亲戚多吗？

2. 你爷爷、奶奶还在吗？他们住在哪儿？

3. 你外公、外婆还在吗？他们住在哪儿？

4. 你有伯伯 / 姑姑 / 叔叔吗？他们有孩子吗？有几个？

5. 你有舅舅 / 阿姨吗？他们有孩子吗？有几个？

6. 你经常跟亲戚见面吗？你们一般什么时候见面？

Report to the class:

他们家亲戚不太多。他爷爷和奶奶现在住在纽约。他外公前年去世了，他外婆现在跟他们一起住。他有一个大伯和一个叔叔。他大伯结婚了，有一个儿子和一个女儿。他叔叔还没有结婚••••••

Extra Words

a) 结婚 jié hūn

b) 离婚 lí hūn

11 Read aloud.

爸爸的爸爸是爷爷，

爸爸的妈妈是奶奶。

爸爸的哥哥是伯父，

爸爸的弟弟是叔叔，

爸爸的姐妹是姑姑。

妈妈的爸爸是外公，

妈妈的妈妈是外婆。

妈妈的兄弟是舅舅，

妈妈的姐妹是阿姨。

12 Listen and tick the right answers.

1	a)前年	b)去年	c)今年
2	a)两个儿子、两个女儿	b)一个儿子、两个女儿	c)三个儿子
3	a)外公、外婆	b)爷爷、奶奶	c)舅舅、姨妈
4	a)中国	b)英国	c)美国
5	a)舅妈	b)姑妈	c)姨妈
6	a)叔叔	b)舅舅	c)伯伯

13 Activity.

Example

爷爷	姨妈	外公	叔叔
阿姨	奶奶	亲戚	孩子
儿子	舅舅	姑姑	外婆
女儿	姐姐	哥哥	伯伯

INSTRUCTIONS

1 The whole class may join the activity.

2 Each student is given a piece of paper with 16 squares. The teacher writes on the board 16 words/phrases, and the students are asked to copy them onto their paper in whatever order they like.

3 The students are asked to tick off the word/phrase the teacher says. Anyone who ticks off four words/phrases in a line in any directions shouts "Bingo"

14 Speaking practice.

Example

我家有爷爷、
奶奶、一个叔叔

It is your turn!

Draw your family tree and introduce your family members to the class.

Text 1

① wǒ jiě jie zhǎng de hěn piào liang　tā guā
我姐姐长得很漂亮。她瓜
zǐ liǎn　yuán yuán de yǎn jing　gāo gāo de bí
子脸，圆圆的眼睛、高高的鼻
zi hé xiǎo xiǎo de zuǐ ba
子和小小的嘴巴。
tā shòu shòu de　tuǐ
她瘦瘦的，腿
cháng cháng de
长长的。

② wǒ gē ge zhǎng de yòu gāo yòu
我哥哥长得又高又
shuài　dàn yǒu diǎnr pàng　tā dà
帅，但有点儿胖。他大
yǎn jing　gāo bí zi　dà zuǐ ba
眼睛、高鼻子、大嘴巴。

NEW WORDS

piào
1. 漂 beautiful

liàng
2. 亮 bright

piào liang
漂亮 beautiful

guā zǐ
3. 瓜子 seeds of sunflower or melon

liǎn
4. 脸(臉) face

guā zǐ liǎn
瓜子脸 oval face

yuán
5. 圆(圓) round

shòu
6. 瘦 thin; slim

yòu
7. 又 also; as well as

yòu　yòu
又…又… both...and...

shuài
8. 帅(帥) handsome

yǒu diǎnr
9. 有点儿 somewhat; rather

pàng
10. 胖 fat; plump

1 Match the picture with the answer.

1

2

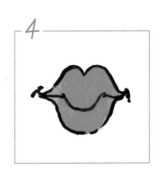

3

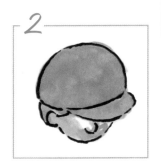

4

5

6

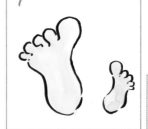

7

8

9

10

NOTE

Some adjectives can be reduplicated for emphasis, e.g.

红红的脸

Answers

a) 大大的眼睛

b) 高高的鼻子

c) 小小的嘴巴

d) 圆圆的头

e) 瘦瘦的脸

f) 胖胖的手

g) 长长的腿

h) 大大的脚

i) 黑黑的头发

j) 大大的耳朵

2 Activity.

INSTRUCTIONS	
1	The whole class may join the activity.
2	When the teacher says the name of a part of the body, every student is expected to point to the right part.
3	Those who point to the wrong part are out of the activity.

Extra Words

yāo
a) 腰

bèi
b) 背

bó zi
c) 脖子

jiān bǎng
d) 肩膀

shǒu zhǐ tou
e) 手指头

jiǎo zhǐ tou
f) 脚趾头

méi mao
g) 眉毛

pì gu
h) 屁股

3 Make a sentence with each group of words given.

1. 高 帅：他长得又高又帅。

2. 矮 瘦：＿＿＿＿＿＿＿＿＿

3. 唱歌 弹钢琴：＿＿＿＿＿＿

4. 发烧 咳嗽：＿＿＿＿＿＿＿

5. 跑步 游泳：＿＿＿＿＿＿＿

6. 中餐 西餐：＿＿＿＿＿＿＿

NOTE

又……又……，means "both...and...", e.g.

今天又刮风又下雨。

4 Activity.

Example

他是男的。他长得很帅。他圆圆的脸、大大的眼睛、高高的鼻子。他的头发……他是谁？

INSTRUCTIONS	
1	The whole class may join the activity.
2	One student describes another student in the class and the rest try to guess who he/she is.

5 Read aloud.

1 yǎnjing 2 bízi 3 zuǐba

4 ěrduo 5 tóufa 6 shétou

7 méimao 8 xiàba 9 pìgu

Practice Focus

Neutral Tone

6 Listen and tick if true, cross if false.

1   2   3   4

7 Make seven sentences following the example.

Example

今天有点儿冷。

| 冷 | 热 | 短 | 矮 |
| 高 | 瘦 | 贵 | 胖 |

NOTE

有点儿 means "somewhat; rather", e.g.

他有点儿胖。

13

8 Describe each of the following people.

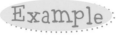

他长得高高的。

他小小的眼睛、

高高的······

他穿······

Sentences for Reference

a) 他长得有点儿胖。

b) 她长得很瘦。

c) 她长得很漂亮。

d) 他长得不好看。

e) 他长得高高的。

f) 他长得又高又帅。

g) 她长得又瘦又小。

h) 她瓜子脸，眼睛大大的。

1

2

9 Memorize the following radicals within 3 minutes.

nǐ dì di zhǎng shén me yàng
你弟弟长什么样？

tā gè zi bù gāo dà gài yǒu mǐ yì mǐ sān
他个子不高，大概有1.3米(一米三)。

tā dà yǎn jing tóu fa duǎn duǎn de shì zhí fà
他大眼睛，头发短短的，是直发。

tā chuān shén me yī fu
他穿什么衣服？

tā chuān hóng hàn shān hé hēi duǎn kù
他穿红汗衫和黑短裤。

tā shì shén me shí hou
他是什么时候

bú jiàn de
不见的？

wǒ mǎi bào zhǐ de shí hou
我买报纸的时候。

nǐ bié zháo jí
你别着急。

wǒ men bāng nǐ zhǎo
我们帮你找。

xiè xie
谢谢！

NEW WORDS

1. 个子 gè zi height; stature
2. 直 zhí straight
3. 是…的 shì de used for emphasis
4. 不见 bú jiàn disappear
5. 报(報) bào report; newspaper
6. 纸(紙) zhǐ paper
   报纸 bào zhǐ newspaper
7. …的时候 de shí hou when
*8. 别 bié don't
9. 着 zháo feel
10. 急 jí anxious
    着急 zháo jí worry
11. 帮(幫) bāng help
12. 找 zhǎo look for

10 Answer the questions.

1. 你做作业的时候会看电视吗？

2. 你上课的时候会说话吗？

3. 你坐车的时候会看书吗？

4. 下大雨的时候你会外出吗？

5. 你吃饭的时候会喝饮料吗？

NOTE

……的时候 means "when", e.g.

我吃饭的时候会看书。

It is your turn!

Make a sentence with "……的时候".

11 Activity.

Example

这是我哥哥。他长得很帅。他大大的眼睛、高高的鼻子……

INSTRUCTIONS

1 | Each student is asked to write about one of his/her family members either in pinyin or in Chinese characters on a piece of paper.

2 | The teacher collects the pieces and shuffles them.

3 | Each student picks one piece and reads it aloud. The rest of the class guess whose family member it describes.

12 Translate from Chinese to English.

1. 你是在哪儿出生的？

2. 他是怎么去北京的？

3. 你是哪年开始学汉语的？

4. 昨天是谁带你去看医生的？

5. 你是什么时候开始发烧的？

6. 这些苹果是在哪儿买的？

NOTE

是……的 emphasizes the past action, time, place, etc., e.g.
A: 你是几点来的？
B: 我是八点来的。

It is your turn!

Make three statements using the "是……的" structure.

13 Say the following in Chinese.

14 Listen and tick the right answers.

1 a)十点半起床　　b)十点半睡觉　　c)七点半上学

2 a)奶奶穿黑衣服　　b)姑姑穿红上衣　　c)姐姐穿黑裤子

3 a)不上学　　b)衣服　　c)女生的校服

4 a)在北京过春节　　b)在上海过圣诞节　　c)在香港过生日

5 a)爷爷、奶奶　　b)亲戚　　c)外公、外婆

6 a)有姑姑和叔叔　　b)女儿、儿子　　c)有姨妈、没有舅舅

15 Speaking practice.

Example

我叫马力，今年十岁，上五年级。我有一个哥哥，他叫马云，今年十四岁，上九年级。我个子不高，大概有1.40米。我喜欢穿汗衫和短裤。我喜欢游泳和跑步。我会弹钢琴、画油画儿。我哥哥个子也不高，大概有1.50米。他……

It is your turn!

Introduce yourself and your siblings.

16 Translate from Chinese to English.

1. 别说话。

2. 别喝可乐。

3. 别出去。

4. 别喝了。

5. 别看电视了。

6. 别玩儿电脑了。

NOTE

别 means "don't", e.g.
别着急。

It is your turn!

Make two sentences with "别".

17 Complete the dialogue with your partner.

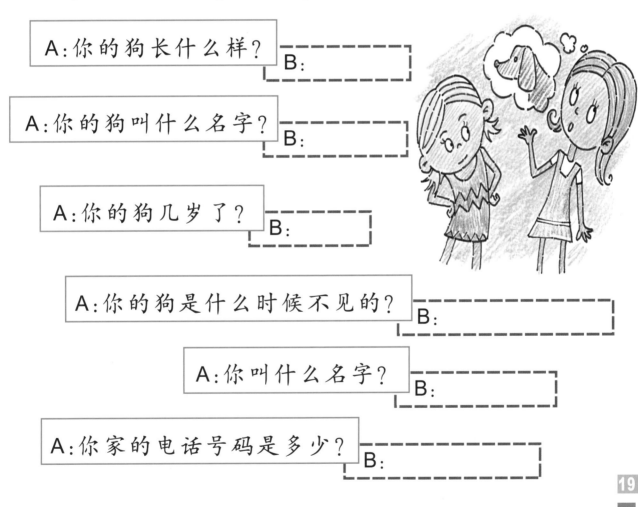

A: 你的狗长什么样？　B:

A: 你的狗叫什么名字？　B:

A: 你的狗几岁了？　B:

A: 你的狗是什么时候不见的？　B:

A: 你叫什么名字？　B:

A: 你家的电话号码是多少？　B:

A: 别着急，我们帮你找。　B:

Text 1

医生： 你哪儿不舒服？
nǐ nǎr bù shū fu

病人： 我头痛、流鼻涕，还拉肚子。
wǒ tóu tòng liú bí tì hái lā dù zi

医生： 你发烧吗？
nǐ fā shāo ma

病人： 不知道。
bù zhī dào

医生： 我给你量一下体温……你发烧了，39.5℃
wǒ gěi nǐ liáng yí xià tǐ wēn   nǐ fā shāo le
（三十九度五）。我给你开一些感冒药。
sān shí jiǔ dù wǔ   wǒ gěi nǐ kāi yì xiē gǎn mào yào
你要多喝水，多休息。
nǐ yào duō hē shuǐ duō xiū xi

病人： 谢谢您。
xiè xie nín

1. 流 ^{liú} flow; run

2. 涕 ^{tì} nasal mucus

   鼻涕 ^{bí tì} nasal mucus

3. 肚 ^{dù} belly; abdomen

   肚子 ^{dù zi} belly; abdomen

拉肚子 ^{lā dù zi} have diarrhoea

4. 给(給) ^{gěi} give; for the benefit of

5. 量 ^{liáng} measure

6. 体温 ^{tǐ wēn} (body) temperature

量体温 ^{liáng tǐ wēn} take somebody's temperature

*7. 开(開) ^{kāi} prescribe

8. 一些 ^{yì xiē} some

9. 药(藥) ^{yào} medicine

---

1 Match the picture with the answer.

1

2

3

4

5

6

7

8

9

Answers

a) 拉肚子

b) 脚疼

c) 发烧

d) 咳嗽

e) 流鼻涕

f) 嗓子疼

g) 量体温

h) 耳朵疼

i) 眼睛疼

2 Activity.

Example

老师：律师

学生1：老师

学生2：商人

学生3：秘书

INSTRUCTIONS

1 | The whole class may join the activity.

2 | The teacher names one item from a particular category, and the students add more to it.

3 | Those who cannot add any or add wrong items are out of the activity.

3 Make dialogues by choosing a sentence from each box.

Example

A: 我发高烧了。

B: 你应该多喝水。

1 我发高烧了。	a) 你应该多喝水。
2 我嗓子疼，今天不能说话。	b) 你应该多穿衣服。
3 我很矮，我想长高。	c) 你应该多运动。
4 我汉语说得不好。	d) 你应该少说话。
5 我很冷。	e) 你应该多休息。
6 我很瘦。	f) 你要少吃米饭。
7 我太胖了。	g) 你要多做练习。
8 我眼睛疼。	h) 你要少看电视。
9 我的数学不好。	i) 你要多吃饭。
10 我今天有点儿不舒服。	j) 你要多练。

4 Memorize the following radicals within 3 minutes.

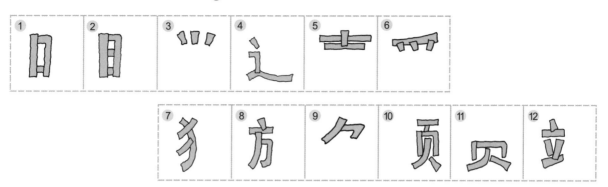

5 Make a similar dialogue with your partner.

A: 下午好！

B: 我叫常青。我是王医生的病人。我今天要去看医生。

A: 下午五点半，可以吗?

B: 太晚了。早一点儿，可以吗?

A: 可以。四点，怎么样?

B: 好。谢谢！再见！

6 Translate from Chinese to English.

1. 开一些药给你

2. 打一个电话给奶奶

3. 买一本书给爸爸

4. 给我做饭

5. 给弟弟穿衣服

6. 给我找一下王老师

> **NOTE**
>
> 给 means "give; for the benefit of", e.g.
> 我给你量一下体温。

It is your turn!

Make a sentence with "给".

7 Read aloud the following and tell the meanings.

1 qīnqi
2 gūgu
3 háizi
4 shūshu
5 péngyou
6 xiānsheng
7 késou
8 xiūxi
9 míngzi
10 xuésheng
11 wǎnshang
12 zěnme
13 yīfu
14 tóufa

8 Listen and tick the right answers.

1
a) 又头痛又拉肚子。
b) 头痛，不发烧。
c) 又咳嗽又发烧。

4
a) 小英今天没上学。
b) 小英去看医生了。
c) 小英上学去了。

2
a) 他流鼻涕。
b) 他发烧了。
c) 他拉肚子了。

5
a) 他发了两天烧。
b) 这两天他感冒了。
c) 他睡了两天觉。

3
a) 外婆生病了。
b) 外公又发烧又咳嗽。
c) 外公头痛。

6
a) 多喝水、少说话
b) 多喝水、少吃饭
c) 多喝水、不吃药

9 Make a sentence with each phrase in the box.

Example

量一下
→我给你量一下体温。

量一下　说一说
看一看　走走
坐坐　等一下

24

mǎ lǎo shī
马老师：

　　nín hǎo
　　您好！

　　wǒ ér zi wáng xiǎo míng zuó tiān xià wǔ tī zú qiú de shí
　　我儿子王小明昨天下午踢足球的时

hou jiǎo shòu shāng le　　　shàng wǔ wǒ dài tā qù kàn yī shēng le
候脚受伤了。上午我带他去看医生了。

yī shēng shuō tā xū yào zài jiā xiū xi liǎng tiān　　suǒ yǐ tā jīn
医生说他需要在家休息两天，所以他今、

míng liǎng tiān bù néng qù shàng xué　　qǐng bìng jià liǎng tiān
明两天不能去上学。请病假两天。

　　　xiè xie
　　　谢谢！

wáng tài tai
王太太

èr yuè shí wǔ rì
二月十五日

NEW WORDS

1. 踢 tī kick
2. 足球 zú qiú football; soccer
3. 受 shòu suffer
4. 伤(傷) shāng wound; injury
   受伤 shòu shāng be injured
5. 需 xū need; require
   需要 xū yào require; want
6. 所 suǒ place; measure word
   所以 suǒ yǐ so
7. 能 néng can; be able to

不能 bù néng cannot; must not
8. 假 jià holiday; leave of absence
   病假 bìng jià sick leave
   请假 qǐng jià ask for leave
   请病假 qǐng bìng jià ask for sick leave

•10 Match the picture with the answer.

1

2   3

4

Answers

a) 他打篮球的时候手受伤了。

b) 他跑步的时候脚受伤了。

c) 他跳远的时候头受伤了。

d) 他跳高的时候腿受伤了。

11 Make a sentence with each dotted word.

1. 你今天应该穿大衣。

2. 爸爸下个月要去北京。

3. 弟弟需要在医院住一个星期。

4. 我可以看电视吗？

5. 不可以在这儿踢球。

6. 明天你能来我家吗？

7. 今天我病了，所以不能去上学。

Practice Focus

a) 应该 should

b) 要 want; need; should; will

c) 需要 require; want

d) 可以 can

e) 不可以 cannot

f) 能 be able to

g) 不能 cannot

12 Complete the telephone conversations.

Example

A: 今天下午妈妈要带我
去看医生，所以我不
能跟你去看电影。

B: 明天上午，可以吗？

A: 可以，我们明天上午
去看电影吧。

B: 好。明天见！

A: 再见！

Situations

A: 姐姐明天上午带我
去看电影，所以我
不能去你家了。

B:

2
A: 哥哥要带我去买东
西，所以我今天下
午不能去踢足球了。

B:

1 a) 他脚痛　　　　b) 他肚子不舒服　　c) 他生病了

2 a) 脚受伤了　　　b) 腿受伤了　　　　c) 头受伤了

3 a) 他昨天没有上学　b) 妈妈生病了　　　c) 妈妈是医生

4 a) 他明天会去上学　b) 请三天病假　　　c) 在家休息两天

5 a) 不用吃饭　　　　b) 需要吃药　　　　c) 多休息

6 a) 他发烧了　　　　b) 他睡觉了　　　　c) 他请假了

14 Activity.

Example

二十年 → 我在上海住了二十年了。

INSTRUCTIONS

1 The whole class may join the activity.

2 Student A picks up a card with a phrase on it, and Student B makes a sentence with the phrase.

3 Those who do not make correct sentences are out of the activity.

《 Samples

一天	两天	五天半
一年	两年	三年半
一个月	三个月	四个半月
一个星期	两个星期	两个半星期
一个上午	一个下午	一个晚上
五分钟	十分钟	一刻钟　一个半小时

15 Role play.

Example

医生：你哪儿不舒服？

病人：我头痛，嗓子也疼。

医生：你从什么时候开始
　　　觉得不舒服的？

病人：下午上英语课的时候。

医生：你发烧了。我给你量
　　　一下体温……三十八
　　　度四。

病人：我明天可以去上学吗？

医生：我给你开一张病假条，
　　　在家休息一天。

Situations

1

咳嗽、拉肚子
39.6℃，不能上学

2

流鼻涕，嗓子疼
38.5℃，休息一天

16 Translate from Chinese to English.

1. 我需要在家休息两天。

2. 奶奶要在我家住半个月。

3. 爸爸要在北京工作一年。

4. 我要请一个星期的病假。

5. 我要吃一个星期的感冒药。

6. 他要画一个下午的画儿。

7. 他每天打两个小时的电话。

It is your turn!

Make two sentences using the grammar "duration of action".

《 Samples

做作业	看电视
游泳	踢足球
睡觉	听音乐

29

Text 1 13

xiāng gǎng yì nián yǒu sì ge jì jié chūn xià qiū dōng
香港一年有四个季节，春、夏、秋、冬。

■ xiāng gǎng de chūn tiān hěn nuǎn huo
香港的春天很暖和，
yǒu shí hou yǒu wù yǒu shí hou
有时候有雾，有时候
hái yǒu léi yǔ qì wēn shí wǔ
还有雷雨，气温十五
dào èr shí wǔ dù
到二十五度。

■ xiāng gǎng de xià tiān hěn rè yǒu
香港的夏天很热，有
shí hou yǒu tái fēng zuì gāo qì
时候有台风，最高气
wēn zài sān shí sān dù zuǒ yòu
温在三十三度左右。

■ xiāng gǎng de qiū tiān tiān qì zuì hǎo
香港的秋天天气最好，
hěn liáng kuai
很凉快。

■ xiāng gǎng de dōng tiān bù lěng zuì
香港的冬天不冷，最
dī qì wēn zài shí dù zuǒ yòu
低气温在十度左右。

New Words

1. 季 _jì_ season
   季节 _jì jié_ season
2. 暖 _nuǎn_ warm

暖和 _nuǎn huo_ nice and warm
3. 雾（霧）_wù_ fog
4. 雷 _léi_ thunder

雷雨 _léi yǔ_ thunderstorm
5. 凉 _liáng_ cool
   凉快 _liáng kuai_ nice and cool

---

1 Say the following in Chinese.

Extra Words

a) 干燥 _gān zào_
b) 潮湿 _cháo shī_
c) 冰雹 _bīng báo_
d) 发大水 _fā dà shuǐ_
e) 龙卷风 _lóng juǎn fēng_
f) 沙尘暴 _shā chén bào_

1
2
3

4
5
6

7
8
9
10

11
12
13
14

15
16
17
18

2 Say a few sentences about each picture.

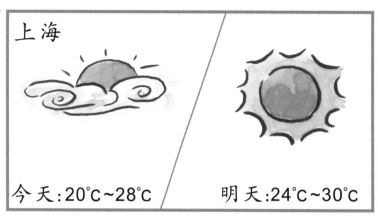

上海

今天：20°C～28°C | 明天：24°C～30°C

Example

上海今天多云，气温二十到二十八度。上海明天天晴，最高温度三十度。

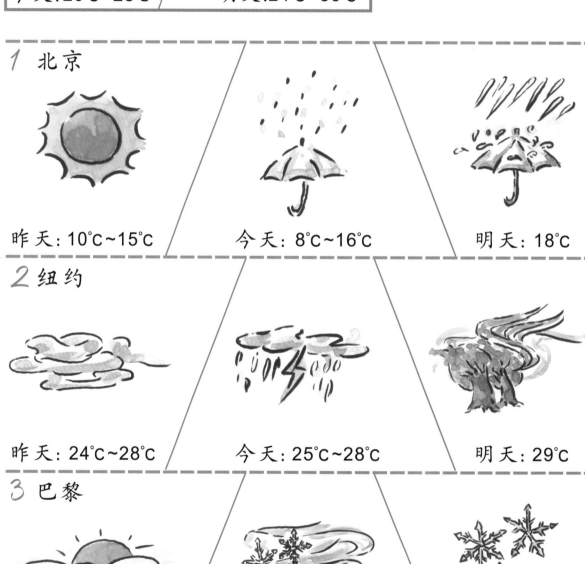

1 北京

昨天：10°C～15°C | 今天：8°C～16°C | 明天：18°C

2 纽约

昨天：24°C～28°C | 今天：25°C～28°C | 明天：29°C

3 巴黎

昨天：-2°C～7°C | 今天：-4°C～5°C | 明天：-4°C

3 Memorize the following radicals within 3 minutes.

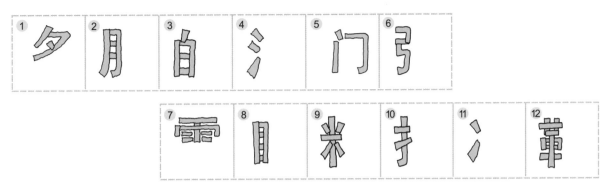

1 夕	2 月	3 自	4 氵	5 门	6 弓
7 雨	8 目	9 米	10 扌	11 冫	12 革

4 Speaking practice.

■ 上海今天多云，最高气温二十八度，最低气温二十度。

■ 明天天晴，气温二十五度到三十度。

■ 后天有毛毛雨，气温在二十度左右。

It is your turn!

Record three days' weather forecasts of a city of your choice.

5 Listen and tick the right answers.

1
a) 春天刮风
b) 夏天下雨
c) 秋天冷

2
a) 下雨
b) 刮台风
c) 下雪

3
a) 纽约冬天下雪
b) 巴黎冬天下雪
c) 伦敦冬天下雪

4
a) 打球
b) 游泳
c) 踢足球

5
a) 听音乐
b) 看电视
c) 看电影

6
a) 脚受伤了
b) 腿受伤了
c) 不舒服

6 Make ten sentences with "最".

Example

加拿大冬天最冷。

a) 冷	h) 大
b) 热	i) 小
c) 长	j) 多
d) 短	k) 少
e) 好	l) 胖
f) 帅	m) 高
g) 漂亮	n) 矮

7 Speaking practice.

Example

北京一年有
四季：春、夏、
秋、冬。北京的
春天不暖和，有
时候气温在十度
左右。北京的夏
天 ......

It is your turn!

Choose a city and introduce its
weather conditions all year round.

34

qīn ài de dōng dong
亲爱的冬冬：

nǐ hǎo
你好！

rú guǒ nǐ shǔ jià lái xiāng gǎng yīng
如果你暑假来香港，应

gāi dài duǎn kù hàn shān hé liáng xié yīn
该带短裤、汗衫和凉鞋，因

wèi xiāng gǎng de xià tiān hěn rè
为香港的夏天很热。

rú guǒ nǐ hán jià lái xiāng gǎng yīng
如果你寒假来香港，应

gāi dài cháng kù máo yī hé wài tào bú
该带长裤、毛衣和外套，不

yòng dài wéi jīn mào zi hé shǒu tào yīn
用带围巾、帽子和手套，因

wèi xiāng gǎng de dōng tiān bú tài lěng nǐ zuì
为香港的冬天不太冷。你最

hǎo dài yì bǎ yǔ sǎn yīn wèi yǒu shí hou
好带一把雨伞，因为有时候

huì xià yǔ
会下雨。

zhù
祝

hǎo
好！

xiǎo tiān
小天

wǔ yuè shí jiǔ rì
五月十九日

NEW WORDS

1. 亲爱 qīn ài dear
2. 如 rú if
   如果 rú guǒ if
3. 暑 shǔ summer
   暑假 shǔ jià summer holidays
4. 鞋 xié shoes
   凉鞋 liáng xié sandals
5. 因 yīn because

6. 为(爲) wèi for (the purpose)
   因为 yīn wèi because
7. 寒 hán cold; chilly
   寒假 hán jià winter holidays
8. 不用 bú yòng need not
9. 围(圍) wéi surround
   围巾 wéi jīn scarf
10. 帽 mào cap; hat

    帽子 mào zi cap; hat
11. 手套 shǒu tào gloves
12. 最好 zuì hǎo had better
13. 伞(傘) sǎn umbrella
    雨伞 yǔ sǎn umbrella
14. 祝 zhù offer good wishes; wish

8 Activity.

Example

老师：毛__

学生1：毛衣

学生2：毛巾

INSTRUCTIONS

1 | The class is divided into small groups.

2 | Each group is asked to add one word to form one or two phrases. The students may write characters if they can, otherwise write *pinyin*.

9 Answer the questions.

1. 如果你今天有五百块，你会怎么花?

2. 如果你今天不上学，你会在家做什么?

3. 如果你今年学五门课，你会学什么?

4. 如果你妈妈今天不做晚饭，你会吃什么?

5. 如果今天下大雪，你会做什么?

NOTE

如果 means "if", e.g.
如果你今晚来我家，我们可以一起玩儿电脑游戏。

It is your turn!

Make a sentence with "如果".

*10 Say the following in Chinese.

Extra Words

a) 西装 (xī zhuāng)

b) 领带 (lǐng dài)

c) 皮带 (pí dài)

d) 皮鞋 (pí xié)

e) 连衣裙 (lián yī qún)

f) 套装 (tào zhuāng)

g) 袜子 (wà zi)

《 Ask your classmates the following questions:

1. 你喜欢什么颜色?

2. 你夏天一般穿什么衣服?

3. 你冬天一般穿什么衣服?

4. 春天,你周末一般穿什么衣服?

5. 你穿什么衣服上学?

6. 你喜欢穿牛仔裤吗?

7. 你爸爸穿什么衣服上班?

8. 你妈妈喜欢穿什么衣服?

11 Complete the sentences.

1. 因为<u>弟弟今天生病</u>，所以他没有去上学。

2. 因为 _____ ，所以我不能外出。

3. 因为 _____ ，所以今天学校都关门。

4. 因为 _____ ，所以我们一家人去饭店吃饭。

5. 因为 _____ ，所以我需要在家休息一个星期。

12 Make a dialogue based on each picture.

13 Listen and tick the right answers.

1
a) 爷爷、奶奶住在日本。
b) 外公、外婆住在日本。
c) 爷爷、奶奶是日本人。

2
a) 姨妈住在德国。
b) 舅舅住在法国。
c) 姑姑住在法国。

3
a) 上海的夏天
b) 上海的春天
c) 上海的秋天

4
a) 北京的天气
b) 北京的四季
c) 北京的冬天

5
a) 带雨衣
b) 穿雨鞋
c) 带雨帽

6
a) 体育课不游泳。
b) 不上体育课了。
c) 体育课打排球。

14 Speaking practice.

Example

A: 冬天去北京，我应该带什么衣服？

B: 你应该带大衣、帽子、围巾、手套等等。

Situations

1. 夏天去纽约　3. 冬天去伦敦

2. 春天去上海　4. 秋天去巴黎

Text 1

① 我爸爸是经理，在一
家英国公司工作。他每天
穿西装、戴领带上班。我
爸爸工作特别忙，还经常
出差。

我妈妈是律师，在一
家美国律师行工作。她喜
欢穿连衣裙和套装。她还
喜欢穿高跟鞋。

②

1. jīng lǐ
   经理 manager

2. sī
   司 manage; department
   gōng sī
   公司 company

3. zhuāng
   装(裝) clothing
   xī zhuāng
   西装 business suit

4. dài
   戴 wear

5. lǐng
   领(領) collar
   lǐng dài
   领带 tie

6. máng
   忙 busy

7. chū chāi
   出差 be on a business trip

8. háng
   行 business firm
   lǜ shī háng
   律师行 law firm

9. lián
   连(連) link; connect
   lián yī qún
   连衣裙 (woman's) one-piece dress

10. tào zhuāng
    套装 woman's suit

11. gāo gēn xié
    高跟鞋 high-heeled shoes

1 Speaking practice.

Example

41

她穿毛衣和长裤。她戴围巾、帽子和手套。

2 Memorize the following radicals within 3 minutes.

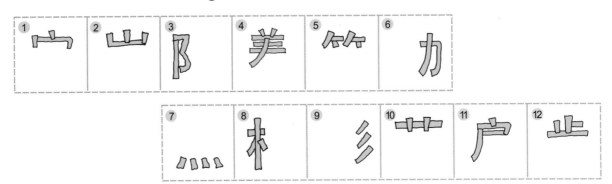

3 Say a few sentences about each picture.

英国人/经理/公司

Example

他是英国人。

他是经理。

他在公司工作。

1

日本人/老师/中学

2

美国人/律师/律师行

3

香港人/秘书/公司

4

西班牙人/商人/公司

5

法国人/画家/大学

6

加拿大人/理发师/理发店

7

澳大利亚人/园丁/公园

4 Activity.

他们最好穿什么衣服？

Example

他上班最好穿西装，戴领带，穿皮鞋。

1. 老师(女): _____

2. 秘书(女): _____

3. 商人(男): _____

4. 医生(男): _____

5. 工人(女): _____

6. 中学生(女): _____

5 Listen and tick the right answers.

1
a) 爸爸在英国工作。
b) 爸爸是工程师。
c) 爸爸在家工作。

2
a) 爸爸每天穿西装上班。
b) 爸爸每天上班。
c) 爸爸有时候穿牛仔裤上班。

3
a) 爸爸今天出差了。
b) 爸爸工作很忙。
c) 爸爸今天很早回家。

4
a) 妈妈是老师。
b) 妈妈是秘书。
c) 妈妈工作不太忙。

5
a) 妈妈爱穿衬衫和裙子。
b) 妈妈每天穿套装上班。
c) 妈妈不喜欢穿连衣裙。

6
a) 他穿校服上学。
b) 他喜欢他的校服。
c) 他穿黑色的长裤。

6 Role play.

你好!

我是小文。你最近忙吗?

我特别忙,每天要做四个小时的作业。

你暑假什么时候来?

大概七月十号左右。

你会来几天?

大约十天。

我们家很大,有四室一厅。你的房间在二楼。

白天我们可以干什么?

我们可以去看电影、逛街,还可以玩儿电脑游戏。

晚上可以干什么?

看电视、看书。

那太好了! 我要去睡觉了。再见!

再见!

It is your turn!

Invite your friend to come over to stay
with you for a period of time.

nín xiǎng mǎi shén me
您想买什么？

wǒ xiǎng mǎi yì shuāng pí xuē
我想买一双皮靴。

nín chuān jǐ hào de xié
您穿几号的鞋？

wǔ hào bàn de wǒ kě yǐ
五号半的。我可以
shì shi zhè shuāng ma
试试这双吗？

dāng rán kě yǐ zěn me yàng
当然可以。……怎么样？
hé shì ma
合适吗？

tǐng hé shì de wǒ hěn xǐ huan
挺合适的，我很喜欢。
duō shao qián
多少钱？

yì qiān liǎng bǎi kuài
一千两百块。

tài guì le wǒ bù mǎi le
太贵了，我不买了。

NEW WORDS

1. 双(雙) pair; measure word
shuāng

2. 皮 leather
pí

3. 靴 boots
xuē

　皮靴 leather boots
pí xuē

4. 试(試) try
shì

5. 当(當) work as
dāng

　当然 of course
dāng rán

6. 合 suit
hé

7. 适(適) fit; suitable
shì

　合适 suitable
hé shì

8. 千 thousand
qiān

9. 太…了 too
tài le

---

7 Make dialogues with your partner.

¥580.00

Example

A: 一双皮鞋多少钱?
B: 五百八十块。

1

¥430.00

2

¥250.00

3

¥800.00

4

¥98.00

5

¥1,250.00

6

¥680.00

7

¥120.00

8

¥25.00

9

¥150.00

10

¥240.00

11

¥65.00

12

¥1,400.00

It is your turn!

List ten things with price tags.

8 Say one sentence about each picture.

Example

我不喜欢穿衬衫。

47

9 Activity.

Measure Words

a) 口 *kǒu*	i) 辆 *liàng*
b) 个 *gè*	j) 门 *mén*
c) 包 *bāo*	k) 位 *wèi*
d) 把 *bǎ*	l) 双 *shuāng*
e) 架 *jià*	m) 套 *tào*
f) 家 *jiā*	n) 张 *zhāng*
g) 条 *tiáo*	o) 本 *běn*
h) 块 *kuài*	p) 节 *jié*

INSTRUCTIONS

1 | The class is divided into small groups.

2 | Each group is asked to match the appropriate measure word with the noun.

3 | The group which has made more correct matches than any other group in the shortest period of time wins.

1. 井	2. 车库	3. 苹果	4. 科学课
5. 床	6. 老师	7. 小说	8. 连衣裙
9. 面粉	10. 手表	11. 皮靴	12. 小提琴
13. 饭店	14. 钢琴	15. 围巾	16. 出租车
17. 飞机	18. 西装	19. 国画儿	20. 汉语课
21. 土豆	22. 杂志	23. 高跟鞋	24. 律师行

10 Say one sentence about each picture.

Example

这条裤子太小了。

NOTE

太……了 means "too", e.g.

这架钢琴太贵了。

1

2

3

4

It is your turn!

Make two sentences with "太……了".

11 Make a similar dialogue with your partner.

¥1500

您想买什么鞋？

我想买一双凉鞋。

您穿几号的鞋？

四号半。

试一下这双。怎么样？

你们有白色的吗？

有，请等一下。……试一下这双。

很舒服，我很喜欢。多少钱？

一千五百块。

太贵了，我不买了。

12 Listen and tick the right answers.

1
a) ¥5,378.00
b) ¥5,738.00
c) ¥8,738.00

4
a) 他应该穿38号的西装。
b) 40号的西装没有了。
c) 38号的西装太小了。

2
a) 连衣裙有三种颜色。
b) 她买了一条红色的。
c) 她不买了。

5
a) 买黑色的皮鞋
b) 一双皮鞋¥580.00
c) 一双皮鞋¥850.00

3
a) 餐桌、椅¥6,500.00
b) 餐桌¥700.00/张
c) 椅子¥700.00/把

6
a) 买领带不可以试。
b) 买围巾可以试。
c) 买帽子不可以试。

Unit 2

Text 1

① 我小时候住在
加拿大。加拿大的
冬天非常冷，常常
下大雪，气温在零
下二十度左右。我
冬天喜欢去滑冰、滑雪。

② 加拿大的夏天不太热，差
不多每天有太阳。我们一家人
喜欢打羽毛球、排球、
网球和乒乓球，有
时候爸爸开车带全
家人去钓鱼。

NEW WORDS

1. xiǎo shí hou 小时候 childhood
2. jiā ná dà 加拿大 Canada
3. huá 滑 slippery; slide
   huá bīng 滑冰 ice-skating
   huá xuě 滑雪 skiing
4. yáng 阳(陽) sun

tài yáng 太阳 sun
5. yǔ 羽 feather
   yǔ máo 羽毛 feather
   yǔ máo qiú 羽毛球 badminton
6. pái 排 line up; row
   pái qiú 排球 volleyball

7. pīng 乒 table tennis
8. pāng 乓 bang
   pīng pāng qiú 乒乓球 table tennis
9. diào 钓(釣) to fish
10. yú 鱼(魚) fish
    diào yú 钓鱼 go fishing

1 List five items for each category.

1. 爱好：	滑冰				
2. 服装：	汗衫				
3. 天气：	晴天				
4. 家人：	爷爷				
5. 生病：	咳嗽				
6. 商店：	书店				

2 Ask your classmates the following questions.

1. 你今年寒假会去滑雪吗？

2. 你这个周末会去滑冰场滑冰吗？

3. 这个周末你会跟爸爸一起去钓鱼吗？

4. 今年圣诞节你会在哪儿过？

5. 你今年暑假会去北京学汉语吗？

3 Memorize the following radicals within 3 minutes.

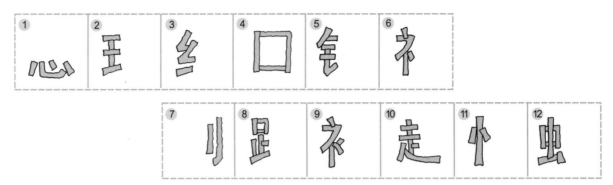

4 Answer the following questions.

我想……

1. 一千年后人会去火星上住吗?

2. 一千年后人出门会坐什么样的车?

3. 一千年后人不用吃饭了吗?

4. 一千年后每个人都会有工作做吗?

5. 一千年后人都不用工作了吗?

6. 一千年后人还会走路吗?

It is your turn!

Draw a picture of a teenager living in a thousand years' time based on your imagination.

5 Make a sentence with each of the dotted words.

Example

1. 我小时候就喜欢跑步。

2. 我有时候晚上十一点睡觉。

3. 我上小学五年级的时候住在上海。

4. 你什么时候回家?

6 Make dialogues with your partner.

Example

A: 中国的古人会跳舞吗?

B: 我想他们会跳舞。

Sentences for Reference
a) 那时候还没有ipod。
b) 中国的古人不会画油画儿。

7 Listen and tick the right answers.

1
a) 他现在住在美国。
b) 他现在住在北京。
c) 他没去过美国。

4
a) 他小时候常钓鱼。
b) 他现在常钓鱼。
c) 他现在住在英国。

2
a) 他会滑雪。
b) 他爱滑冰。
c) 他住在加拿大。

5
a) 他昨天去滑雪了。
b) 他昨天去滑冰了。
c) 他跟朋友一起去滑雪了。

3
a) 他打网球。
b) 他不打羽毛球。
c) 他打乒乓球。

6
a) 现在是冬天。
b) 现在正在下雨。
c) 现在正在刮风。

8 Speaking practice.

Example

我小时候住在上海。那时候上海的冬天很冷，经常下雪，气温在零下十度左右。我们家没有电视机，也没有暖气，所以冬天的晚上我们很早就睡觉了。

那时候上海的夏天很热，常常是晴天，有时候有雷雨，气温在三十度左右。我每天都去游泳。

It is your turn!

Talk about the weather and activities you used to do when you were a child.

我小时候住在……

那里的冬天……

我冬天常常……

那里的夏天……

我夏天常常……

wǒ yào mǎi yì tiáo yùn dòng kù yí jiàn yóu yǒng yī hé
我要买一条运动裤、一件游泳衣和
jǐ shuāng wà zi wǒ hái xiǎng zài mǎi yì dǐng mào zi
几双袜子。我还想再买一顶帽子。

wǒ men jiā mào zi tài duō le bú yào zài mǎi le
我们家帽子太多了，不要再买了。

wǒ néng bu néng mǎi yí fù ěr huán
我能不能买一副耳环？

nǐ yǐ jīng yǒu èr shí fù ěr huán le bú yào zài mǎi le
你已经有二十副耳环了，不要再买了。

mā ma zhè tiáo xiàng liàn hěn hǎo kàn wǒ kě bu kě yǐ mǎi yì tiáo
妈妈，这条项链很好看。我可不可以买一条？

zhè tiáo xiàng liàn yào yí wàn wǔ qiān kuài tài guì le
这条项链要一万五千块，太贵了。

NEW WORDS

1. jiàn 件 measure word

2. yóu yǒng yī 游泳衣 swimming suit

*3. jǐ 几(幾) several

4. wà 袜(襪) socks
   wà zi 袜子 socks

5. dǐng 顶(頂) measure word; top

6. fù 副 measure word

7. huán 环(環) ring; loop
   ěr huán 耳环 earring

8. yǐ 已 already

9. yǐ jīng 已经 already

10. xiàng 项(項) nape (of the neck)

11. liàn 链(鏈) chain
    xiàng liàn 项链 necklace

12. wàn 万(萬) ten thousand

9 Say the following in Chinese.

Example

一条连衣裙

1 2 3 4 5 6 7 8 9 10 11 12 13

56

10 Activity.

Example

A:不要再<u>看电视</u>了。

B:那好吧，我出去打球。

看电视	睡觉	说	喝
打电话	踢球	试	买

INSTRUCTIONS

1 | The class is divided into pairs.

2 | Each pair is expected to make a dialogue following the example according to the action word given by the teacher.

3 | The pair which fails to make a logical dialogue is out of the activity.

11 Listen and tick the right boxes.

24

	手套	游泳衣	运动裤	袜子	帽子	耳环	项链	围巾
1								
2								
3								
4								
5								
6								

12 Match the two parts to make a sentence.

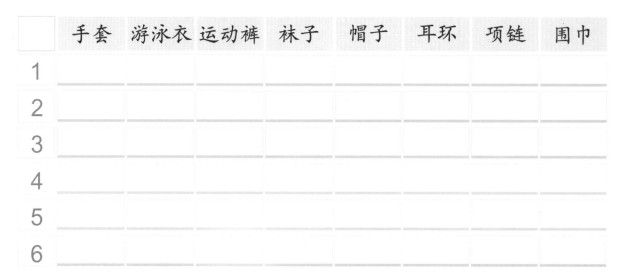

A

_____ 1 他坐上午九点的飞机去北京，

_____ 2 他九点就上床了，

_____ 3 小明今天不能来上学，

_____ 4 王红吃了一个月的中药，

B

a)我想他已经睡了。

b)我想她的病已经好了。

c)我想他已经到了吧。

d)我已经知道了。

It is your turn!

Make a sentence with "已经".

57

13 Make dialogues with your classmates.

Example

A：我能不能看看这条项链？

B：当然可以。

A：不好看。……我可不可以试一下这件外套？

B：可以。

A：这件外套多少钱？

B：两千块。

A：太贵了，我不买了。

¥12,000.00

1
¥220.00

2
¥350.00

¥2,000.00

4
¥420.00

3
¥2,400.00

8

5
¥250.00

6
¥130.00

7
¥260.00

¥1,200.00

9
¥1,500.00

10
¥800.00

11
¥5,000.00

12
¥120.00

14 Role play.

Example

妈妈:这双靴子怎么样?
　　我喜欢这双。
售货员:您穿几号的鞋?

Situations

你跟妈妈一起去买东西。
你想买……

- 一双运动鞋,八号,白色
  大概想花¥400.00
- 一件毛衣,十四号,棕色
  大概想花¥300.00
- 一条牛仔裤,十号,黑色
  大概想花¥150.00

Questions for Reference

a) 您想买什么?

b) 我能帮您吗?

c) 您穿几号的鞋?

d) 我可以试一下这件吗?

e) 你们有黑色的吗?

f) 这件怎么样? 合适吗?

g) 这双鞋多少钱?

15 Activity.

Verbs:

穿　戴　打　量
看　买　滑　……

Nouns:

领带　　项链
冰　　　西装
体温　　报纸
羽毛球　……

INSTRUCTIONS

1　The class is divided into groups of 3 or 4.

2　The teacher gives out two sets of cards. There are verbs on one set of cards, and nouns on the other. The students are asked to match the verbs with the nouns to form phrases. They need to write down the phrases in correct characters.

3　The group which makes the most correct phrases is the winner.

Text 1

wǒ jīn nián xué shí mén kè   yīng wén   hàn yǔ   yīn yuè   shù xué
我今年学十门课：英文、汉语、音乐、数学、

diàn nǎo   wù lǐ   huà xué
电脑、物理、化学、

shēng wù   dì lǐ hé lì
生物、地理和历

shǐ   wǒ xǐ huan shàng lì
史。我喜欢上历

shǐ kè   yīn wèi lǎo shī
史课，因为老师

duì wǒ hěn hǎo   wǒ duì
对我很好，我对

lì shǐ hěn gǎn xìng qù
历史很感兴趣。

wǒ yě xǐ huan xué hàn
我也喜欢学汉

yǔ   yīn wèi wǒ jué
语，因为我觉

de hàn yǔ hěn yǒu yòng
得汉语很有用。

dàn shì hàn yǔ hěn nán
但是汉语很难

xué   yīn wèi hàn zì
学，因为汉字

bù róng yì xiě
不容易写。

1. 物 wù thing
   物理 wù lǐ physics
   生物 shēng wù biology
2. 化 huà change
   化学 huà xué chemistry
3. 地理 dì lǐ geography
4. 对…好 duì hǎo nice to
5. 感 gǎn feel; sense
6. 兴(興) xìng mood; interest
7. 趣 qù interest
   兴趣 xìng qù interest
   对…感兴趣 duì gǎn xìng qù be interested in
8. 觉得 jué de feel
9. 有用 yǒu yòng useful
10. 难(難) nán difficult
11. 容 róng hold; contain
12. 易 yì easy
    容易 róng yì easy
13. 写(寫) xiě write

1 Comment on each subject.

Example

我觉得英语很有用。
英语也不难学。

Sentences for Reference

a) 我觉得汉语很有用。

b) 我觉得物理很难学。

c) 我觉得化学不太难学。

d) 我觉得地理不难学。

e) ……，所以我喜欢学汉语。

f) 化学不容易学。

g) 汉字很难写。

1

2

5

3

Français

4

6

7

8

9

10

11

12

13

2 Memorize the following characters within 3 minutes.

① 东	② 南	③ 西	④ 北	⑤ 木	⑥ 禾
⑦ 石	⑧ 山	⑨ 光	⑩ 土	⑪ 足	⑫ 舌

3 Speaking practice.

星期一	
8:00-8:45	数学
8:45-9:00	课间休息
9:00-9:45	汉语
9:45-10:00	课间休息
10:00-10:45	化学
10:45-11:00	课间休息
11:00-11:45	物理
11:45-13:15	午休
13:15-14:00	音乐
14:00-14:15	课间休息
14:15-15:00	英语

Example

我今年学十门课：英语、汉语、数学、化学、物理、地理等。我每天上六节课。我们八点开始上课。我上午上四节课。我中午十一点三刻吃午饭。我下午再上两节课。我们三点放学。

It is your turn!

Tell the class about yourself following the example.

4 Activity.

Example

英文	数学	体育	电脑	美术
法语	历史	日语	音乐	物理
地理	化学	生物	汉语	戏剧

INSTRUCTIONS

1 The class is divided into two groups.

2 The teacher puts up 10-16 flash cards on the board. The students are given 2-3 minutes to memorize them.

3 Then the teacher takes off one word/phrase card secretly and asks the students to tell the missing word/phrase.

5 Comment on each subject and teacher.

Example

因为我对数学很
感兴趣，数学老
师对我很好，所
以我喜欢学数学。

Sentences for Reference

a) 汉语老师对我很好。

b) 我对电脑很感兴趣。

1 2 3 4 5

6 7 8 9 10

Français

6 Listen and choose the right letters.

	A	觉得语言容易学。
___ 1 小东	B	对历史感兴趣。
___ 2 小明	C	的数学老师对他好。
___ 3 小文	D	觉得生物很难学。
___ 4 大生	E	觉得化学很有趣。
___ 5 小天	F	觉得英语很有用。
___ 6 小雪	G	对音乐不感兴趣。
	H	觉得地理课很有意思。
	I	的戏剧老师不好。

7 Make a dialogue with your partner.

《 Sample questions:

1. 你今年多大了？上几年级？

2. 你今年学几门课？哪几门课？

3. 你喜欢上什么课？为什么？

4. 你喜欢哪个老师？为什么？

5. 你觉得汉语难学吗？

6. 你喜欢学汉语吗？

7. 你有什么爱好？

8. 你不喜欢做什么？

9. 你周末一般做什么？

nǐ xǐ huan xué nǎ ge kē mù
你喜欢学哪个科目？

wǒ zuì xǐ huan huà xué
我最喜欢化学。

wèi shén me
为什么？

yīn wèi wǒ jué de huà xué hěn yǒu yì si　lǎo shī jiāo de　yě hǎo
因为我觉得化学很有意思，老师教得也好。

nǐ měi tiān gōng kè duō ma　yào zuò duō cháng shí jiān
你每天功课多吗？要做多长时间？

bú tài duō　dà gài yào zuò liǎng ge xiǎo shí
不太多，大概要做两个小时。

nǐ men cháng cháng yǒu cè yàn　kǎo shì ma
你们常常有测验、考试吗？

měi ge yuè cè yàn yí cì　měi ge xué qī kǎo liǎng sān cì
每个月测验一次，每个学期考两三次。

NEW WORDS

1. 科目 (kē mù) subject; course
2. 为什么 (wèi shén me) why
3. 意 (yì) meaning
4. 思 (sī) think
   意思 (yì si) meaning

有意思 (yǒu yì si) interesting
5. 教 (jiāo) teach
6. 功 (gōng) achievement
   功课 (gōng kè) homework
7. 测(测) (cè) measure

8. 验(験) (yàn) test
   测验 (cè yàn) test
9. 考 (kǎo) give or take an examination
   考试 (kǎo shì) examination
10. 学期 (xué qī) semester

8 Give appropriate answers to the questions.

1. 你昨天为什么没有来上学？ 因为我昨天病了。

2. 你为什么喜欢学汉语？

3. 你为什么每年要去美国过圣诞节？

4. 你为什么喜欢冬天？

5. 你为什么这个周末不能来我家？

6. 你为什么不喜欢吃蔬菜？

It is your turn!

Each group of three students makes four questions with "为什么" and then ask other groups to answer them.

9 Activity.

Example

学生A：对……感兴趣
学生B：我对物理不感兴趣。

INSTRUCTIONS

1 The whole class may join the activity.

2 Student A picks up a card with a phrase on it, and Student B makes a sentence with the phrase.

3 Those who do not make correct sentences are out of the activity.

10 Translate from Chinese to English.

1. 我有五六个中国朋友。

2. 这条牛仔裤要一两百块钱。

3. 我的数学老师有四十五六岁。

4. 他发烧了，有三十八九度。

5. 你应该在家休息一两个月。

6. 姐姐有八九条连衣裙。

7. 妈妈有二三十副耳环。

8. 我去过英国三四次。

It is your turn!

Make three sentences using the same grammar.

11 Ask your partner the following questions.

1. 什么科目有意思？

2. 什么科目没有意思？

3. 什么科目难学？

4. 什么科目容易学？

5. 哪个老师教得好？

6. 哪个老师教得不好？

7. 哪个老师对学生好？

8. 哪个老师对学生不好？

9. 哪个科目有用？

10. 哪个科目没用？

| Report to the class:

他觉得数学、地理和化学课很有意思。

他觉得 ......

12 Listen and tick the right answers.

1. a) 她学十门课　　b) 她学戏剧　　c) 她不学体育

2. a) 她喜欢数学　　b) 她不喜欢化学　　c) 她最喜欢科学

3. a) 中学一年级　　b) 小学一年级　　c) 小学三年级

4. a) 汉语有用　　b) 汉语难学　　c) 汉语没有意思

5. a) 物理老师教得好　　b) 她不喜欢学物理　　c) 物理不容易学

6. a) 功课很多　　b) 考试不多　　c) 每天有功课

13 Make a sentence with each group of words given.

Example

化学老师　教　→　我的化学老师教得很好。

汉语老师　弹钢琴　→　我的汉语老师钢琴弹得很好。

1. 姑姑　滑冰　→
2. 妹妹　跳远　→
3. 弟弟　跑步　→
4. 姐姐　弹钢琴　→
5. 叔叔　说汉语　→
6. 哥哥　打篮球　→
7. 爸爸　打乒乓球　→
8. 妈妈　打羽毛球　→
9. 爷爷　画国画儿　→

14 Make five questions and then ask your partner to answer them.

1. 你打了多长时间电话?

2. 你会在上海住几天?

3. 你每天游几个小时的泳?

4. 你每天晚上睡几个小时的觉?

5. 你每天做几个小时的作业?

15 Speaking practice.

Example

我叫万思文，今年上十一门课，有英文、汉语、化学、物理、生物、地理等。我喜欢上科学和数学课，因为我对理科感兴趣。老师对我都很好，他们也教得很好。我不喜欢学语言，因为英语和汉语都很难，但是我知道它们很有用。

It is your turn!

Introduce yourself.

16 Interview your partner.

≪ Sample questions:

1. 你在哪个学校上学？你喜欢你的学校吗？

2. 你们学校有多少老师？多少学生？

3. 你觉得你们学校的老师怎么样？他们教得好吗？

4. 你们每天功课多吗？一般要做多长时间？

5. 你们经常有测验吗？你们一个学期有几次考试？

6. 你喜欢学语言吗？你觉得汉语难学吗？

Report to the class:

他在京西中学上学。他喜欢 ......

Text 1

wǒ lái jiè shào
我来介绍

yí xià wǒ men xué xiào
一下我们学校。

wǒ men xué xiào jiào nán
我们学校叫南

shān yīng wén xué xiào
山英文学校。

xué xiào yǒu wǔ zhuàng jiào
学校有五幢教

xué lóu　　yí ge tú
学楼、一个图

shū guǎn　　yí ge lǐ
书馆、一个礼

táng　　yí ge cāo chǎng
堂、一个操场、

yí ge tǐ yù guǎn
一个体育馆、

liǎng ge lán qiú chǎng hé
两个篮球场和

yí ge zú qiú chǎng
一个足球场。

xué xiào hái yǒu yí ge
学校还有一个

cān tīng　　yí ge yóu
餐厅、一个游

yǒng chí hé yí ge tíng
泳池和一个停

chē chǎng
车场。

餐厅　操场　足球场　图书馆　游泳池　篮球场　教学楼　礼堂　停车场　南山英文学校

70

NEW WORDS

1. 介 jiè introduce
2. 绍(紹) shào introduce
   介绍 jiè shào introduce
3. 幢 zhuàng measure word
4. 教学 jiào xué teaching
5. 图(圖) tú picture; drawing
6. 馆(館) guǎn place; building

图书馆 tú shū guǎn library
7. 礼(禮) lǐ ceremony; ritual
8. 堂 táng main room of a house
   礼堂 lǐ táng auditorium
9. 操 cāo exercise
   操场 cāo chǎng playground
10. 体育馆 tǐ yù guǎn gymnasium

11. 篮球场 lán qiú chǎng basketball court
12. 足球场 zú qiú chǎng football pitch
13. 池 chí pool
   游泳池 yóu yǒng chí swimming pool
14. 停车场 tíng chē chǎng parking lot

---

1 Say a few sentences about each picture.

图书馆

Example

这是图书馆。图书馆里有很多书。
有些学生在看书，有些学生在看杂志。

1···教学楼	2···操场	3···礼堂	4···体育馆

5···餐厅	6···足球场	7···音乐室	8···游泳池

2 Activity.

1. 操 <u>场</u>　2. ___期　3. 意___

4. 功___　5. ___果　6. 游___

7. 时___　8. ___装　9. 凉___

10. 公___　11. ___带　12. 杂___

13. 钓___　14. ___环　15. ___经

16. 考___　17. ___假　18. ___理

19. 围___　20. ___药　21. ___球

INSTRUCTIONS

1　The class is divided into small groups.

2　Each group is asked to add one word to form a phrase. The students may write characters if they can, otherwise write *pinyin*.

3　The group which makes the most correct phrases is the winner.

3 Speaking practice.

我来介绍一下我们学校。
我们学校有……

游泳池　后门　图书馆　礼堂　操场　足球场　篮球场　餐厅　体育馆　停车场　教学楼

4 Listen and tick the right answers.

1 a)学校有礼堂。
　　b)学校有六幢教学楼。
　　c)学校有图书馆。

4 a)中午打篮球。
　　b)中午打排球。
　　c)中午踢足球。

2 a)公共图书馆有十层。
　　b)学校图书馆在十层。
　　c)学校体育馆在一层。

5 a)学校有游泳池。
　　b)学校的足球场不小。
　　c)学校有体育馆。

3 a)礼堂有两层。
　　b)礼堂在楼下。
　　c)礼堂在一楼。

6 a)学校离他家不远。
　　b)学校离他家不近。
　　c)学校不在他家附近。

5 Activity.

1.杂志( )　2.帽子( )　3.耳环( )

4.袜子( )　5.钢琴( )　6.沙发( )

7.外套( )　8.西装( )　9.长发( )

10.围巾( )　11.节目( )　12.商店( )

13.青菜( )　14.汽车( )　15.语言( )

16.老师( )　17.小狗( )　18.椅子( )

19.项链( )　20.衬衫( )　21.桌子( )

INSTRUCTIONS

1　The class is divided into small groups.

2　Each group is asked to write a measure word that matches the noun.

3　The group has made more correct matches than any other group in certain period of time wins.

6 Speaking practice.

Example

这是我们的汉语教室。教室里有白板、桌子 ......

现在教室里有七个人。老师跟一个学生 ......

Extra Words

a) 铅笔 (qiān bǐ)   e) 白板 (bái bǎn)

b) 钢笔 (gāng bǐ)   f) 卷笔刀 (juǎn bǐ dāo)

c) 尺子 (chǐ zi)   g) 练习本 (liàn xí běn)

d) 橡皮 (xiàng pí)   h) 计算器 (jì suàn qì)

It is your turn!

Go to one of the classrooms and describe what you see.

新生1： hàn yǔ jiào shì zài jǐ céng
汉语教室在几层？

小明： zài sān céng　　zài fǎ yǔ jiào shì de páng biān
在三层，在法语教室的旁边。

新生2： wù lǐ shí yàn shì zài nǎr
物理实验室在哪儿？

小明： zài yī hào jiào xué lóu de èr céng　　zài yīn yuè shì de gé bì
在一号教学楼的二层，在音乐室的隔壁。

新生1： cè suǒ zài nǎr
厕所在哪儿？

小明： zài yī lóu　　nán cè suǒ zài zuǒ bian　　nǚ cè suǒ zài yòu bian
在一楼。男厕所在左边，女厕所在右边。

新生2： xiào zhǎng bàn gōng shì zài nǎr
校长办公室在哪儿？

小明： zài wǔ hào jiào xué lóu yī céng　　zài jiào shī bàn gōng shì hé xiào yī shì de zhōng jiān
在五号教学楼一层，在教师办公室和校医室的中间。

NEW WORDS

1. jiào shì 教室 classroom
2. sān céng = sān lóu 三层=三楼 third floor
3. páng biān 旁边 side
4. shí 实(實) true
   shí yàn 实验 experiment
   shí yàn shì 实验室 laboratory
5. gé 隔 separate

6. bì 壁 wall
   gé bì 隔壁 next door
7. nán 男 male
8. cè 厕(厠) toilet
   cè suǒ 厕所 toilet
9. zuǒ bian 左边 left side
10. yòu bian 右边 right side

11. xiào zhǎng 校长 principal
12. bàn 办(辦) do
    bàn gōng 办公 work
    bàn gōng shì 办公室 office
13. jiào shī 教师 teacher
14. xiào yī shì 校医室 school clinic
15. zhōng jiān 中间 between; centre

· **7** Speaking practice.

Example 钢琴在床对面。

Words for Reference

a) 上面/边

b) 下面/边

c) 左面/边

d) 右面/边

e) 前面/边

f) 后面/边

g) 对面

h) 旁边

It is your turn!

Ask your partner to draw your room while you are describing it.

8 Memorize the following characters within 5 minutes.

① 米	② 豆	③ 果	④ 瓜	⑤ 角	⑥ 田
⑦ 食	⑧ 虫	⑨ 鸟	⑩ 羊	⑪ 今	⑫ 天

9 Speaking practice.

Example

实验室在四楼。图书馆在实验室右面。

Words for Reference

a) 楼上

b) 楼下

c) 左面

d) 右面

e) 隔壁

f) 中间

It is your turn!

Draw one of the teaching blocks of your school and describe it to the class.

10 Listen and tick the right answers.

1 a) 图书馆在六层。

 b) 图书馆在二层。

 c) 图书馆在教学楼旁边。

2 a) 化学实验室在二楼。

 b) 化学实验室在一楼。

 c) 化学实验室在楼下。

3 a) 超市在一层。

 b) 超市在楼上。

 c) 厕所在超市的二层。

4 a) 校长办公室在中间。

 b) 图书馆在中间。

 c) 教师办公室在中间。

5 a) 他们在图书馆。

 b) 他们在实验室。

 c) 他们在礼堂。

6 a) 音乐室不在二楼。

 b) 美术室在二楼。

 c) 电脑室在一层。

11 Activity.

1	女	石	⺌	巾	饣	欠	火
2	又	矢	牛	車	日	辶	艹
3	罒	豸	方	勹	灬	页	贝
4	立	夕	月	自	氵	门	弓
5	米	目	寺	冫	革	宀	屮
6	阝	羊	竹	力	灬	木	彡
7	艹	户	肉	心	纟	至	钅
8	礻	刂	跟	衤	走	忄	虫

INSTRUCTIONS

1 The class is divided into small groups.

2 Each group is asked to write radicals. The group writing more correct radicals than any other group in certain period of time wins.

上海飞机场

和平大饭店

青青花店

上海火车站

大光明电影院　金光家具店

民生书店

百家超市

上海第一人民医院

四季服装店

加油站

方圆文具店

Example

飞机场在和平大饭店左边。青青花店在和平大饭店右边。电影院在

市中心图书馆

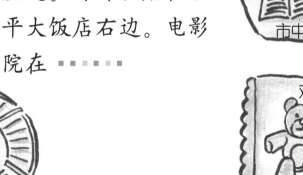

上海体育馆

欢欢玩具店

It is your turn!

Redesign your city centre, draw the layout and describe it to the class.

Text 1 🔘33

wǒ men xué xiào yǒu yí ge wén jù diàn　　lǐ bian yǒu qiān bǐ
我们学校有一个文具店，里边有铅笔、

chǐ zi　xiàng pí　juǎn bǐ dāo　liàn xí běn　rì jì běn
尺子、橡皮、卷笔刀、练习本、日记本、

wén jù hé děng　chú le zhè xiē　wén jù diàn hái mài xiǎo shuō
文具盒等。除了这些，文具店还卖小说、

kè běn　kǎ piàn děng　wén
课本、卡片等。文

jù diàn zài wǔ hào jiào
具店在五号教

xué lóu li　zài yī
学楼里，在一

lǒu　nǐ yí jìn
楼。你一进

xiào mén jiù néng
校门就能

kàn jiàn
看见。

NEW WORDS

1. 里边=里面 (lǐ biān / lǐ miàn) inside
2. 铅(鉛) (qiān) lead
3. 笔(筆) (bǐ) pen
   铅笔 (qiān bǐ) pencil
4. 尺 (chǐ) ruler
   尺子 (chǐ zi) ruler
5. 橡 (xiàng) rubber
   橡皮 (xiàng pí) rubber; eraser
6. 卷 (juǎn) curl

卷笔刀 (juǎn bǐ dāo) pencil sharpener
7. 练(練) (liàn) practise
   练习 (liàn xí) practise
8. 本 (běn) book
   练习本 (liàn xí běn) exercise book
   课本 (kè běn) textbook
9. 记(記) (jì) remember; record
   日记 (rì jì) diary
   日记本 (rì jì běn) diary (book)

10. 盒 (hé) box; case
    文具盒 (wén jù hé) pencil case
11. 小说 (xiǎo shuō) novel
12. 卡 (kǎ) card
13. 片 (piàn) piece
    卡片 (kǎ piàn) card
14. 一…就… (yī... jiù...) as soon as
15. 进(進) (jìn) enter
16. 看见 (kàn jiàn) see

---

1 Describe the picture.

Example

铅笔在书桌上。课本 ⋯⋯⋯

Words for Reference

a) 铅笔
b) 钢笔
c) 尺子
d) 橡皮
e) 卷笔刀
f) 练习本
g) 日记本
h) 课本
i) 卡片
j) 文具盒

2 Say one sentence about each picture.

图书馆

Example

你一进学校
大门就可以
看见图书馆。

NOTE

1. 一……就…… means "as soon as", e.g.
   他一放学就回家。
2. Complement of result, e.g.
   你一进房门就可以看见一个大书柜。

1

客厅

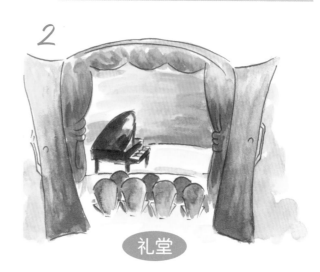

2

礼堂

3

It is your turn!

Make a sentence containing
"一……就……" and "看见".

厨房

3 Memorize the following characters within 5 minutes.

❶ 目	❷ 足	❸ 心	❹ 舌	❺ 叉	❻ 勺
❼ 巾	❽ 血	❾ 皿	❿ 刀	⓫ 包	⓬ 豆

4 Guess the meaning of each phrase.

	看	听	找	买	吃	做	喝	卖
1 见	看见 see	听见						
2 到	看到	听到	找到	买到				
3 光					吃光		喝光	卖光
4 好				买好	吃好	做好		

Example

1. 我昨天看见他姐姐了。
2. 我听到弟弟在楼上踢球。
3. 我买到运动鞋了。
4. 我找到了我的手机。

It is your turn!

Choose four words from above and make a sentence with each of them.

5 Listen and tick the right boxes.

34

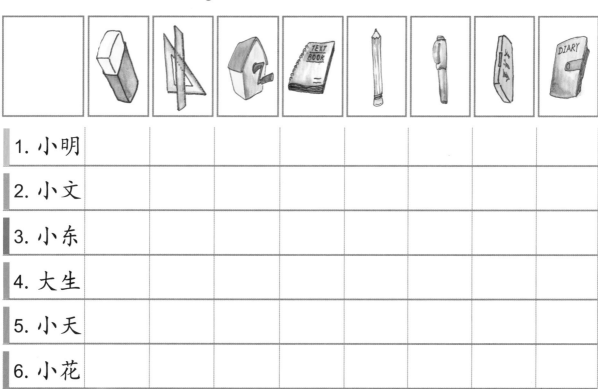

				TEXT BOOK				DIARY
1. 小明								
2. 小文								
3. 小东								
4. 大生								
5. 小天								
6. 小花								

Extra Words

a) 支 zhī

b) 礼品纸 lǐ pǐn zhǐ

c) 钢笔 gāng bǐ

d) 毛笔 máo bǐ

e) 笔记本 bǐ jì běn

Example

A：一本汉语课本多少钱？

B：一百一十八块。

A：一支铅笔多少钱？

B：三块九毛。

A：一共多少钱？

B：一百二十一块九毛。

A：给你一百五十块。

B：找你二十八块一毛。

Situations

You have ¥200.00 and you would like to buy some stationery items in this shop.

nǐ yǒu qiān bǐ ma
你有铅笔吗?

yǒu
有。

wǒ jīn tiān wàng jì dài qiān bǐ le   jiè
我今天忘记带铅笔了。借

gěi wǒ yì zhī yòng yí xià   xíng ma
给我一支用一下,行吗?

xíng
行。

jiè nǐ de jì suàn qì yòng yí xià   kě yǐ ma
借你的计算器用一下,可以吗?

wǒ yí huìr jiù huán gěi nǐ
我一会儿就还给你。

duì bu qǐ   wǒ zhèng yòng ne
对不起,我正用呢。

nǐ gēn bié de tóng xué jiè ba
你跟别的同学借吧。

hǎo ba
好吧。

85

NEW WORDS

1. 忘 wàng forget
   忘记 wàng jì forget
2. 借 jiè borrow; lend
3. 支 zhī measure word
*4. 行 xíng be all right

5. 计(計) jì calculate
   计算 jì suàn calculate
6. 器 qì instrument
   计算器 jì suàn qì calculator
*7. 就 jiù as early as; right away

*8. 还(還) huán return
*9. 别 bié other
10. 同 tóng same
    同学 tóng xué classmate

---

7 Say the following in Chinese.

Example

笔记本

1

2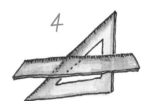

3

4

5

6

7

8

9

10

11

12

13

14

8 Say the following in Chinese.

Example

一支铅笔

9 Translate from Chinese to English.

1. 我现在上厕所，行吗？

2. 我现在看电视，可以吗？

3. 我等一会儿吃晚饭，行吗？

4. 我想买这条项链，可以吗？

5. 我不吃中药，行吗？

6. 我今晚十二点睡觉，可以吗？

7. 我不去钓鱼，行吗？

NOTE

行 means "be all right", e.g.
  A: 我今晚去你家，行吗？
  B: 不行。我晚上要去看电影。

It is your turn!

Make two questions and ask your classmates to answer them.

10 Role play.

Example

A: 借我二十块钱，行吗？我忘记带钱包了。我明天还给你。

B: 好吧，别忘了明天还给我。

借……

a) 二十块钱
b) 一块橡皮
c) 一把尺子
d) 一本汉语课本
e) 一个手机
f) 一本杂志
g) 一个计算器

11 Group discussion.

你会借给别人手机吗？会。/ 不会。

你会借给别人的东西	你不会借给别人的东西
● 铅笔 ●	● 游泳衣 ●
● ●	● ●
● ●	● ●
● ●	● ●

12 Make dialogues with your classmates.

Example

A: 你会借铅笔给别人吗？

B: 会。

A: 你会跟别人借钱吗？

B: 不会。

a) 铅笔　　f) 钱
b) 尺子　　g) 手机
c) 橡皮　　h) 毛衣
d) 书包　　i) 运动鞋
e) 课本　　j) 牛仔裤

13 Listen and tick the right answers.

1 a) 忘带日记本　　b) 忘带笔记本　　c) 忘带练习本

2 a) 借英语课本　　b) 借汉语课本　　c) 借数学课本

3 a) 借手机　　b) 借电脑　　c) 借计算器

4 a) 借文具盒　　b) 借钢笔　　c) 借铅笔

5 a) 忘带书包　　b) 忘带钱包　　c) 忘带文具盒

6 a) 没带运动衣　　b) 没带运动鞋　　c) 没带运动裤

14 Role play.

Example

| a) 手机 ¥2,300 | b) 铅笔 ¥0.80 | c) 计算器 ¥120 |
| d) 电脑 ¥9,400 | e) 苹果 ¥10/4个 | f) 小说 ¥68 |

顾客：这个手机多少钱？

售货员：两千三百块。

顾客：我可以看看吗？

售货员：当然可以。······ 你喜欢吗？

顾客：很喜欢。我买了。给你 两千五百块。

售货员：找你两百块。

Text 1 37

wǒ jiā fù jìn
我家附近

yǒu yí ge cài shì chǎng
有一个菜市场，

nà li mài xīn xiān zhū
那里卖新鲜猪

ròu　niú ròu　jī ròu
肉、牛肉、鸡肉、

huó yú　huó xiā
活鱼、活虾、

dòu fu　hái mài gè
豆腐，还卖各

zhǒng xīn xiān shū cài hé
种新鲜蔬菜和

shuǐ guǒ
水果。

wǒ mā ma tè
我妈妈特

bié xǐ huan qù shì chǎng
别喜欢去市场

mǎi cài tā shuō nà li
买菜。她说那里

de cài bǐ chāo shì li
的菜比超市里

de xīn xiān　hái pián
的新鲜，还便

yi　zài cài shì chǎng
宜。在菜市场，

yì gōng jīn píng guǒ bā
一公斤苹果八

kuài qián　zài chāo shì
块钱，在超市

yào mài shí èr kuài qián
要卖十二块钱。

NEW WORDS

shì chǎng
1. 市场 market

cài shì chǎng
2. 菜市场 fresh market

xīn
3. 新 new

xiān
4. 鲜(鮮) fresh

xīn xiān
新鲜 fresh

zhū
5. 猪 pig

ròu
6. 肉 meat

zhū ròu
猪肉 pork

niú ròu
牛肉 beef

jī
7. 鸡(鷄) chicken

jī ròu
鸡肉 chicken meat

huó
8. 活 alive; live

xiā
9. 虾(蝦) shrimp

fǔ
10. 腐 short for bean curd

dòu fu
豆腐 tofu; bean curd

gè
11. 各 all; every

bǐ
12. 比 compare

yí
13. 宜 suitable

pián yi
便宜 cheap

gōng jīn
14. 公斤 kilogram

---

1 Say the following in Chinese.

大白菜
¥2.50/斤

Example

大白菜两块五毛一斤。

1
土豆
¥1.50/斤

2
南瓜
¥3.00/斤

3
西红柿
¥3.10/斤

4
冬瓜
¥1.30/斤

5
豆角
¥2.80/斤

6
菜花儿
¥3.00/斤

7
黄瓜
¥2.10/斤

8
活鱼
¥15.00/条

9
活虾
¥15.00/斤

10
猪肉
¥10.00/斤

11
羊肉
¥12.00/斤

12
牛排
¥14.00/斤

13
鸡翅/鸡腿
¥13.00/斤

14
豆腐
¥1.50/块

15
豆腐干
¥1.00/块

2 Memorize the following characters within 5 minutes.

① 金	② 匕	③ 亡	④ 尸	⑤ 丁	⑥ 入
⑦ 户	⑧ 井	⑨ 弓	⑩ 方	⑪ 习	⑫ 皿

3 Say one sentence about each picture.

水果店

Example

这家水果店（卖）各种新鲜水果。

他们卖 ·······

1

服装店

2

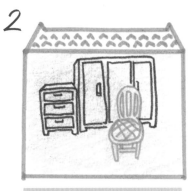

家具店

3

中药店

4

书店

5

电器店

6

文具店

4 Complete the following sentences.

1. 牛肉比 ＿＿＿＿＿＿＿＿ 好吃。

2. 我的书包比 ＿＿＿＿＿＿＿ 便宜。

3. 今年夏天比 ＿＿＿＿＿＿＿ 热。

4. 这双凉鞋比 ＿＿＿＿＿＿ 舒服。

5. 这个空调比 ＿＿＿＿＿＿＿ 小。

It is your turn!

Make two sentences with "比".

5 Role play.

Example

老师：这双运动鞋是你的吗?

学生：不是。我的是白色的。

老师：这双白色的是不是你的?

学生：也不是。我的比这双新。

老师：这双新的运动鞋是你的吗?

学生：就是这双。谢谢!

6 Listen and write down the prices.

	猪肉	牛排	羊肉	鸡腿	活鱼	活虾	豆腐
1							
2							
3							
4							
5							
6							

7 Speaking practice.

Example

上个星期天我跟妈妈一起去菜市场买菜了。我们买了：
- 一斤半猪肉
- 一斤青菜
- 一条活鱼
- 两斤西红柿

我们一共花了三十六块五毛。我们经常去这个菜市场买菜，因为那里的菜比超市的新鲜，还便宜。

It is your turn!

Describe one of your shopping experiences.

¥5.50
¥7.60
¥10.00
¥1.50
¥15.00
¥16.00

nǐ měi tiān wǔ fàn chī shén me
你每天午饭吃什么？

wǒ yǒu shí hou cóng jiā li dài sān
我有时候从家里带三
míng zhì yǒu shí hou zài xué xiào
明治，有时候在学校
cān tīng mǎi dōng xi chī
餐厅买东西吃。

nǐ píng shí mǎi xiē shén me
你平时买些什么？

wǒ tōng cháng mǎi hé fàn chī yǒu shí
我通常买盒饭吃，有时
hou yě huì mǎi shǔ piàn shǔ tiáo
候也会买薯片、薯条、
zhá jī chì bǎng táng guǒ děng
炸鸡翅(膀)、糖果等。

hé fàn guì ma duō shao qián yì hé
盒饭贵吗? 多少钱一盒?

shí jiǔ kuài bú suàn tài guì
十九块，不算太贵。

nǐ xǐ huan chī nǎ zhǒng hé fàn
你喜欢吃哪种盒饭?

wǒ cháng mǎi gā lí niú ròu fàn yú liǔ fàn zhū pái fàn děng
我常买咖喱牛肉饭、鱼柳饭、猪排饭等。

NEW WORDS

1. 三明治 *sān míng zhì* sandwich
2. 平 *píng* usual
   平时 *píng shí* usually
3. 盒饭 *hé fàn* box lunch
4. 薯 *shǔ* potato; yam
   薯片 *shǔ piàn* chips; crisps

5. 炸 *zhá* deep-fry
6. 翅 *chì* wing
7. 膀 *bǎng* shoulder
   翅膀 *chì bǎng* wing
8. 糖 *táng* sugar

薯条 *shǔ tiáo* French fries

糖果 *táng guǒ* candy; sweets
9. 咖喱 *gā lí* curry
10. 柳 *liǔ* willow
    鱼柳 *yú liǔ* fish fillet
11. 猪排 *zhū pái* pork chop

---

8 Say the following in Chinese.

糖果 ¥5.80

Example

一卷糖果五块八毛。

薯条 ¥5.50

3

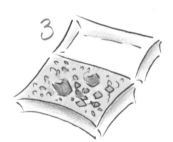
咖喱牛肉盒饭 ¥15.00

1
三明治 ¥15.00

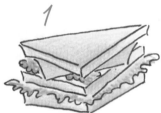
炸鸡腿 ¥8.40

4

5
炸鸡翅 ¥10.00

6
薯片 ¥7.60

7
鱼柳盒饭 ¥16.00

8
猪排盒饭 ¥14.00

It is your turn!

List 4 types of food and drinks each with a price tag.

9 Activity.

1. 办公室
2. 西装
3. 领带
4. 连衣裙
5. 耳环
6. 足球
7. 计算器
8. 帽子
9. 手套
10. 电冰箱
11. 大楼
12. 语言
13. 三明治
14. 汽车
15. 电炉
16. 游泳池
17. 钢琴
18. 电池
19. 烤箱
20. 报纸
21. 围巾
22. 豆腐
23. 蔬菜
24. 校服
25. 项链
26. 电脑
27. 小狗
28. 薯片
29. 皮靴
30. 椅子

INSTRUCTIONS

1 | The class is divided into small groups.

2 | Each group is asked to find appropriate measure words to match the nouns.

3 | The group which has made more correct matches than any other group in the shortest period of time is the winner.

10 Listen and choose the right letters.

_____ 1 学校有

_____ 2 餐厅卖

_____ 3 午饭有

_____ 4 盒饭

_____ 5 她午饭常吃

_____ 6 她常喝

A	各种饮料。
B	炸鸡翅。
C	一家餐厅。
D	十九块一盒。
E	热狗。
F	饮料。
G	盒饭。
H	炸鸡腿。
I	三明治。

•11 Make dialogues with your partner.

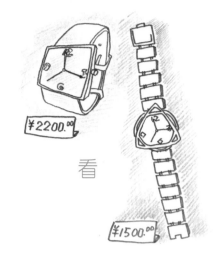

¥2200.00

看

¥1500.00

Example

售货员：你想看哪块手表？

顾客：这块，一千五百块的。

1···买

¥10.00/条

2···买

¥2.18/斤

3···买

¥65.00/个

¥85.00/个

4···试穿

¥50.00/条

¥186.00/条

5···看

¥145.00/条

¥130.00/副

6···买

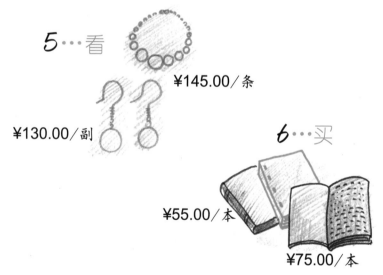

¥55.00/本

¥75.00/本

7···试穿

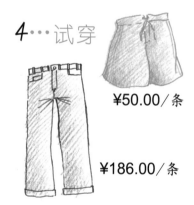

¥580.00/双

¥465.00/双

8···看

¥150.00/条

¥126.00/条

12 Complete the sentences.

1. 我平时 <u>八点到学校</u> ，但是 <u>今天七点就到了</u> 。

2. 我通常 <u>   </u> ，但是 <u>   </u> 。

3. 我一般 <u>   </u> ，但是 <u>   </u> 。

4. 我有时候 <u>   </u> ，但是 <u>   </u> 。

5. 我经常 <u>   </u> ，但是 <u>   </u> 。

13 Interview your partner.

« Sample questions:

1. 你早上一般几点起床？你早饭一般吃什么？

2. 你一般几点上学？你怎么上学？

3. 你们上午上几节课？下午上几节课？

4. 你们中午几点吃午饭？你一般吃什么？

5. 你们学校有餐厅吗？你经常去那里买什么吃？

6. 你们下午几点放学？你一般几点到家？

7. 你们家平时几点吃晚饭？吃什么？

8. 你晚上一般在家做什么？你一般几点睡觉？

| Report to the class:

他早上一般六点半起床。

他早饭一般吃 ......

99

Text 1 41

wǒ tè bié xǐ huan chī líng shí　wǒ měi tiān dōu chī gè zhǒng
我特别喜欢吃零食。我每天都吃各种

gè yàng de líng shí　bǐ rú　táng guǒ　qiǎo kè lì　shǔ piàn
各样的零食，比如：糖果、巧克力、薯片、

dàn gāo　bīng qí lín
蛋糕、冰淇淋、

bǐng gān děng　wǒ hái xǐ
饼干等。我还喜

huan hē qì shuǐ　wǒ zhī
欢喝汽水。我知

dao táng guǒ hé qì shuǐ duì
道糖果和汽水对

yá chǐ bù hǎo　kě shì
牙齿不好，可是

wǒ cóng xiǎo jiù xǐ huan chī
我从小就喜欢吃

líng shí　mā ma zǒng shì
零食。妈妈总是

duì wǒ shuō　bú yào chī
对我说，不要吃

tài duō líng shí　yīng gāi
太多零食，应该

duō chī zhèng cān
多吃正餐。

NEW WORDS

1. 零食 líng shí snack
2. 各种各样 gè zhǒng gè yàng all kinds of
3. 比如 bǐ rú for example
4. 巧克力 qiǎo kè lì chocolate
5. 蛋 dàn egg
6. 糕 gāo cake

7. 蛋糕 dàn gāo cake
8. 冰淇淋 bīng qí lín ice cream
9. 饼干 bǐng gān cookies; cracker
10. 牙 yá tooth
11. 齿(齒) chǐ tooth
12. 牙齿 yá chǐ tooth

11. 从小 cóng xiǎo from childhood
12. 总(總) zǒng always
13. 总是 zǒng shì always
14. 正餐 zhèng cān lunch or supper; dinner

---

1 Say a few sentences about each picture.

Example

我以前非常喜欢吃三明治。我每天午饭吃三明治。我自己会做三明治。可是我现在喜欢吃盒饭了，比如咖哩牛肉饭、猪排饭等等。

Phrases for Reference

a) 非常喜欢
b) 特别喜欢
c) 挺喜欢
d) 最喜欢
e) 不太喜欢

1 鸡翅 鸡腿

2 猪肉 牛肉 羊肉

3 水果 薯片

4 巧克力 糖果

5 冰淇淋 饮料

6 蛋糕 饼干

7 西红柿 黄瓜

8 香蕉 苹果

101

2 Complete the sentences.

1. 我特别喜欢买衣服，比如连衣裙、汗衫、毛衣、牛仔裤等。

2. 我很喜欢_____

3. 我非常喜欢_____

4. 我_____

5. 我_____

3 Add more items to each category.

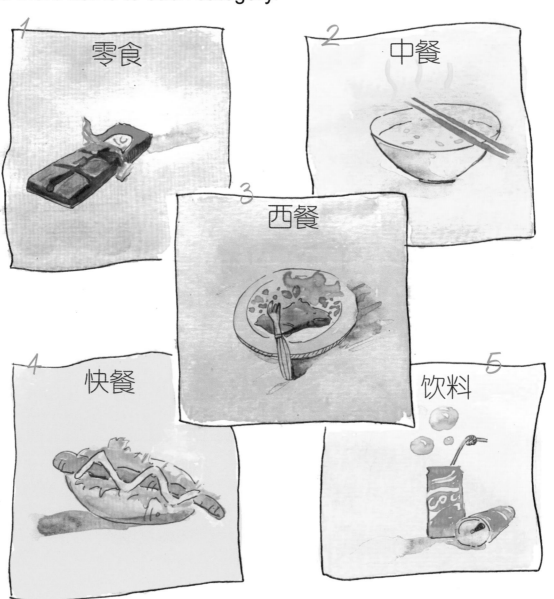

1 零食

2 中餐

3 西餐

4 快餐

5 饮料

4 Complete the sentences.

1. 我对 ＿＿＿＿＿＿＿＿＿＿＿＿ 非常感兴趣。

2. 多吃糖果对 ＿＿＿＿＿＿＿＿＿＿ 不好。

3. 我们学校的老师都对 ＿＿＿＿＿＿＿＿＿＿ 很好。

4. 我对 ＿＿＿＿＿＿＿＿＿＿ 一点儿都不感兴趣。

5. ＿＿＿＿＿＿＿＿＿＿ 对 ＿＿＿＿＿＿＿＿＿＿＿＿。

5 Say one sentence about each picture.

超市

Example

这家超市卖各种各样的零食，比如巧克力、糖果等。

1···服装店

2···肉店

3···水果店

4···餐厅

5···文具店

6···家具店

7···电器店

103

1 她喜欢 _____。
   a) 在学校买零食
   b) 从市场上买糖果
   c) 自己做蛋糕

4 她从小喜欢吃 _____。
   a) 主食
   b) 糖果
   c) 水果

2 她吃 _____。
   a) 巧克力和糖果
   b) 蛋糕和饼干
   c) 糖果和薯片

5 她晚饭 _____。
   a) 吃得多
   b) 吃得少
   c) 不吃

3 她喝 _____。
   a) 水和可乐
   b) 汽水
   c) 牛奶

6 她每天有 _____。
   a) 四十块零用钱
   b) 三十块零用钱
   c) 三十四块零用钱

7 Speaking practice.

Example

我从小就喜欢吃零食，比如蛋糕、巧克力、薯片、糖果等。我从小就喜欢喝可乐。我每天都要喝可乐，因为我不喜欢喝白开水。我从小就喜欢弹钢琴。我现在钢琴弹得很好，已经考过了五级。我从小就 • • • • • •

It is your turn!

Make a similar introduction of yourself.

nǐ zǎo fàn chī shén me
你早饭吃什么？

chī gǔ lèi zǎo cān jiā niú nǎi　yǒu shí
吃谷类早餐加牛奶，有时
hou chī miàn bāo　jiān dàn hé xiāng cháng
候吃面包、煎蛋和香肠。

wǔ fàn ne
午饭呢？

chī sān míng zhì　rè gǒu　suān nǎi　yǒu shí
吃三明治、热狗、酸奶，有时
chī shǔ tiáo　zá cài tāng　shā lā děng
吃薯条、杂菜汤、沙拉等。

nǐ men jiā wǎn fàn chī shén me
你们家晚饭吃什么？

yǒu shí hou chī zhōng cān
有时候吃中餐，
yǒu shí hou chī xī cān
有时候吃西餐。

nǐ men jiā píng shí shuí zuò
你们家平时谁做
fàn　nǐ huì bāng máng ma
饭？你会帮忙吗？

yì bān shì mā ma zuò
一般是妈妈做。
yǒu shí hou chī wán wǎn
有时候吃完晚
fàn yǐ hòu　wǒ huì
饭以后，我会
bāng mā ma xǐ wǎn
帮妈妈洗碗。

NEW WORDS

1. 谷(穀) gǔ cereal; grain

   类(類) lèi kind; type

   谷类 gǔ lèi cereal

2. 加 jiā add; plus

3. 牛奶 niú nǎi milk

4. 面包 miàn bāo bread

5. 煎 jiān fry in shallow oil

6. 肠(腸) cháng intestine

   香肠 xiāng cháng sausage

7. 酸 suān sour

   酸奶 suān nǎi yoghurt

8. 有时 yǒu shí = 有时候 yǒu shí hou sometimes

9. 汤(湯) tāng soup

   杂菜汤 zá cài tāng vegetable soup

10. 沙拉 shā lā salad

11. 帮忙 bāng máng help

12. 完 wán finish

13. 碗 wǎn bowl

---

8 Say a few sentences about each picture.

Example

我喜欢吃薯条。

我每天都吃薯条。

1

2

3

4

5

6

7

8

9

10

11

12

13

14

9 Interview four classmates with the questions below.

QUESTIONS	NOTES
1. 你早饭一般吃什么？	
2. 你午饭一般吃什么？	
3. 你晚饭一般吃什么？	
4. 你们家周末常常去饭店吃饭吗？	
5. 你们一般去哪家饭店吃饭？	
6. 你们在饭店一般吃什么？	

Report to the class:

三个同学早饭一般吃水果和面包，喝牛奶。一个同学有时候早饭吃谷类早餐加牛奶。午饭他们一般吃盒饭。两个同学家晚饭一般吃 ⋯⋯⋯⋯

10 Ask your partner the following questions.

1. 我有时候在学校餐厅买午饭吃，你呢？

2. 你小时候在哪儿住过？

3. 上课的时候你可以吃东西吗？

4. 放学以后，你一般什么时候到家？

5. 你从小就喜欢吃什么？不喜欢吃什么？

It is your turn!

Make a question with each of the dotted words.

11 Complete the sentences.

1. 我吃完早饭以后 _刷牙_ 。

2. 他游完泳以后去 _____ 。

3. 我们一家人看完电影以后去 _____ 。

4. 她做完作业以后去 _____ 。

5. _____ 帮妈妈洗碗。

6. _____ 跟姐姐一起去买菜。

7. _____ 去图书馆看书。

8. _____ 跟爸爸一起去钓鱼。

NOTE

……完……以后，……
means "after finishing",
e.g.

做完作业以后，他
看电视。
＝他做完作业以后看
电视。

It is your turn!

Make three sentences with
the structure "……完……
以后，……".

12 Listen and choose the right answers.

44

1 今天早餐她想吃 _____ 。
a) 面包、煎蛋
b) 谷类早餐加牛奶
c) 牛奶、面包

2 她想在她的茶里加 _____ 。
a) 糖和牛奶
b) 水和糖
c) 牛奶

3 她今天午饭想吃 _____ 。
a) 汉堡包和薯条
b) 炸鸡腿和沙拉
c) 炸鸡翅和沙拉

4 她昨天晚饭吃了 _____ 。
a) 杂菜汤、水果和面包
b) 比萨饼和沙拉
c) 杂菜汤、沙拉和面包

5 他们家一般吃 _____ 。
a) 西餐
b) 中餐
c) 快餐

6 他们家平时 _____ 。
a) 她做饭，妈妈洗碗
b) 妈妈做饭，妈妈洗碗
c) 妈妈做饭，她洗碗

13 Memorize the following characters within 5 minutes.

① 矢	② 斗	③ 力	④ 寸	⑤ 青	⑥ 旦
⑦ 自	⑧ 己	⑨ 亡	⑩ 立	⑪ 几	⑫ 上

14 Project.

INSTRUCTION

Design a menu for your school canteen. It should be in a pamphlet form.

学校餐厅菜单

早餐	午餐	晚餐
•	•	•
•	•	•
•	•	•
•	•	•
•	•	•

Unit 4

Text 1

wǒ men yì jiā sān kǒu shàng ge zhōu mò qù chī zì zhù cān le　wǒ

我们一家三口上个周末去吃自助餐了。我

men chī le lóng xiā　sān wén yú　shòu sī　kǎo niú pái　chǎo miàn děng

们吃了龙虾、三文鱼、寿司、烤牛排、炒面等。

wǒ men hái chī le hěn duō tián pǐn　yǒu nǎi lào　qiǎo kè lì dàn gāo hé

我们还吃了很多甜品，有奶酪、巧克力蛋糕和

shuǐ guǒ shā lā　wǒ men dōu chī de hěn bǎo　wǒ men yí gòng huā le sān

水果沙拉。我们都吃得很饱。我们一共花了三

bǎi duō kuài　tǐng pián yi de

百多块，挺便宜的。

NEW WORDS

zhù
1. 助 help

zì zhù cān
   自助餐 buffet

lóng
2. 龙(龍) dragon

lóng xiā
   龙虾 lobster

sān wén yú
3. 三文鱼 salmon

shòu sī
4. 寿司 sushi

kǎo
5. 烤 bake; roast

niú pái
6. 牛排 beefsteak

tián
7. 甜 sweet

pǐn
8. 品 article; goods

tián pǐn
   甜品 dessert

lào
9. 酪 thick fruit juice

nǎi lào
   奶酪 cheese

bǎo
10. 饱(飽) full

1 Describe the picture.

主食

甜品

Example

在这个自助餐厅，主食你可以吃到龙虾 • • • • • •

甜品你可以吃到奶酪蛋糕 • • • • • •

Memorize the following characters within 5 minutes.

① 包	② 止	③ 夕	④ 平	⑤ 反	⑥ 习
⑦ 页	⑧ 欠	⑨ 贝	⑩ 革	⑪ 乌	⑫ 勺

3 Make a similar dialogue with your partner.

Example

A: 我们星期天下午去红山饭店吃自助餐了。

B: 你们吃了什么? 喝了什么?

A: 我们吃了甜点, 有蛋糕、饼干、冰淇淋等。我们还吃了寿司、炒面和炒饭。

B: 有水果吗?

A: 当然有。我们吃了西瓜、苹果和香蕉。

B: 在那里吃饭贵不贵?

A: 还可以, 每位一百五十块。

4 Complete the sentences.

1. 我一般喝完汤以后再 ___吃主食___ 。

2. 我一般吃完主食以后再 _____ 。

3. 我一般踢完球以后 _____ 。

4. 我一般做完 _____ 。

5. 我一般 _____ 。

It is your turn!

Make two sentences with "完……以后……".

5 Role play.

售货员：我能帮你吗？

顾客：我想买几个龙虾。多少钱一个？

售货员：六十块。

顾客：挺贵的。

售货员：不算贵，已经很便宜了。

顾客：我觉得很贵。我不买了。

Situations

You are supposed to buy food
for your family with ￥200.00.

 龙虾 ￥60.00/个

 三文鱼 ￥68.00/块

 寿司 ￥5.00/个

 鸡腿 ￥12.00/斤

 活鱼 ￥12.00/条

 牛排 ￥22.00/斤

 活虾 ￥25.00/斤

 鸡翅 ￥10.00/斤

 香肠 ￥18.00/斤

6 **Listen and choose the right answers.**

1 他们家一般 ___ 去吃一次。
a) 一周
b) 两周
c) 一个月

4 那家饭店 ___ 。
a) 烤牛排做得最好吃
b) 烤羊排做得不好吃
c) 烤猪排做得一般

2 他们家常去吃 ___ 。
a) 西式自助餐
b) 中式自助餐
c) 日本料理

5 那家饭店的饭菜 ___ 。
a) 又不好吃又贵
b) 又好吃又便宜
c) 做得好吃，但是挺贵的

3 上个周末 ___ 。
a) 她爸爸病了
b) 她妈妈病了
c) 她自己不舒服

6 下个月 ___ 。
a) 爸爸要出差
b) 爸爸回来
c) 妈妈要出差

7 **Speaking practice.**

Example

上个星期天是我妈妈的生日。我们一家四口去了一家自助餐厅吃晚饭。我们吃了龙虾、三文鱼、寿司、烤牛排等。我们还吃了各种甜品，比如巧克力蛋糕、奶酪蛋糕等。爸爸买了一个生日蛋糕。我们一起给妈妈唱了生日歌。我们每个人都吃得很饱。爸爸一共花了六百多块，挺便宜的。

It is your turn!

Describe your recent eating-out experience.

爸爸

wǒ men dōu hěn è le wǒ men xiàn
我们都很饿了。我们现
zài jiù diǎn lái bàn zhī kǎo yā
在就点。来半只烤鸭、
yí ge chǎo ròu sī yí ge hóng shāo
一个炒肉丝、一个红烧
dòu fu yí ge zhēng yú zài lái
豆腐、一个蒸鱼。再来
yí ge chǎo qīng cài
一个炒青菜。

服务员

gè wèi hǎo zhè shì cài
各位好，这是菜
dān qǐng wèn kě yǐ
单……请问可以
diǎn cài le ma
点菜了吗?

服务员

yào bu yào mǐ fàn
要不要米饭?

爸爸

lái sān wǎn mǐ fàn ba
来三碗米饭吧。

服务员

qǐng wèn xiǎng hē diǎnr shén me
请问，想喝点儿什么?

爸爸

lái liǎng bēi lǜ chá zài lái liǎng píng kě lè
来两杯绿茶，再来两瓶可乐。

NEW WORDS

dān
1. 单(單) bill

cài dān
菜单 menu

diǎn cài
2. 点菜 order food
(in a restaurant)

è
3. 饿(餓) hungry

zhī
4. 只(隻) measure word

yā
5. 鸭(鴨) duck

kǎo yā
烤鸭 roast duck

sī
6. 丝(絲) silk; thread

ròu sī
肉丝 shredded meat

shāo
7. 烧(燒) cook

hóng shāo
红烧 braise in soy sauce

zhēng
8. 蒸 steam

qīng cài
9. 青菜 green vegetables

bēi
10. 杯 cup

chá
11. 茶 tea

lǜ chá
绿茶 green tea

píng
12. 瓶 bottle

---

8 Say a few sentences about each picture.

龙虾

Example

我非常喜欢吃龙虾。

我每个月吃一次龙虾。

1
奶酪蛋糕

2
白巧克力

3
寿司

4
烤鸭

5
红烧豆腐

6
蒸鱼

7
炒青菜

8
烤牛排

9
水果沙拉

10
绿茶

11
香肠

12
薯条

13
青豆蛋炒饭

14
冰淇淋

9 Activity.

1. 瓶：___ ___
2. 杯：___ ___
3. 辆：___ ___
4. 本：___ ___
5. 节：___ ___
6. 件：___ ___
7. 位：___ ___
8. 只：___ ___
9. 家：___ ___
10. 张：___ ___
11. 斤：___ ___
12. 个：___ ___
13. 双：___ ___
14. 包：___ ___

INSTRUCTIONS

1 The class is divided into small groups.

2 Each group is asked to find two nouns to match each measure word.

3 The group which has made more correct matches than any other group in the shortest period of time is the winner.

10 Make a dialogue with your partner.

服务员 | 晚上好！家乐快餐店。

小明 | 我想叫外卖。

服务员 | 请说。

 x 4

小明 | 来一个比萨饼、四个炸鸡腿、两个汉堡包和四瓶可乐。一共多少钱？

服务员 | 一百五十六块。

Situations

Order a lunch for a group of five people over the telephone.

117

11 Interview your partner.

	QUESTIONS	NOTES
1	你喜欢吃中餐吗？喜欢吃什么？	
2	你喜欢吃西餐吗？喜欢吃什么？	
3	你喜欢吃自助餐吗？你常去吃吗？	
4	你喜欢吃快餐吗？喜欢吃什么？	
5	你早饭一般吃什么？	
6	你午饭一般吃什么？	
7	你晚饭一般吃什么？	
8	你一般喜欢喝什么？	
9	你上个周末去饭店吃饭了吗？	
10	你去了哪家饭店？吃了什么？	
11	你一共花了多少钱？	

Report to the class:

她喜欢吃中餐。她特别喜欢吃蒸鱼和豆腐。她也喜欢吃西餐。她非常喜欢吃烤牛排。她也喜欢吃自助餐。她每个月去吃一次自助餐。她还喜欢吃快餐。她喜欢吃……

12 Listen and choose the right letters.

___ 1 小天	A	午饭时吃水果。
___ 2 小文	B	不常吃快餐。
___ 3 小山	C	中午在学校买盒饭吃。
___ 4 冬冬	D	爱吃西瓜和梨。
___ 5 小云	E	晚饭时常吃蔬菜。
___ 6 小明	F	很胖，因为常吃快餐。
	G	爱吃巧克力、冰淇淋、薯片等。
	H	一家人常去饭店吃北京烤鸭。

13 Make dialogues with your classmates.

Example

A: 薯片多少钱一包？

B: 四块五。

A: 买两包。给你十块。

B: 找你一块。

Situations

Suppose you are a shop owner selling food/drinks.

14 Complete the dialogue.

Example

服务员：各位好，这是菜单……
请问可以点菜了吗？

爸爸：可以。来……

NOTE

要，点 and 来 are used to order food in a restaurant, e.g.

A: 几位点什么菜？
B: 来（要）半只烤鸭。

服务员：几位想喝什么？

爸爸：……

快乐自助餐厅	天天快餐店	北京饭店	欢欢茶餐厅
龙虾	热狗	烤鸭	蛋炒饭
寿司	汉堡包	红烧豆腐	鱼蛋面
烤牛排	比萨饼	蒸鱼	炒面
沙拉	香肠	炒肉丝	白粥
巧克力蛋糕	煎蛋	炒青菜	鱼片粥
各种水果、甜品	可乐	炒大虾	绿茶
果汁	汽水		

Example

这家饭店叫中港西餐馆，一共有两层。一楼有十张餐桌，可以坐下五十个人。二楼有十二张餐桌，可以坐下六十个人。厨房在一楼。男、女厕所一楼、二楼都有。在这家饭店你可以吃到......

INSTRUCTIONS

1 | This can be a joint project managed by two students or a small group.

2 | Each group is expected to draw the layout of the restaurant on an A4 size paper, and write up the menu of the restaurant on a separate piece of paper.

3 | The class together with the teacher judge each project based on the design, the quality of the drawing and the language used.

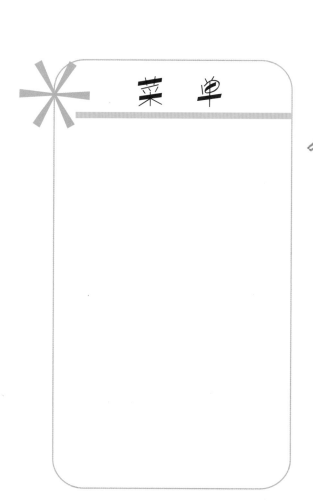

菜　单

Text 1

wǒ jiā zhù zài shì zhōng xīn　shēng huó hěn fāng biàn　yóu jú lí wǒ jiā
我家住在市中心，生活很方便。邮局离我家

bù yuǎn　chāo jí shì chǎng jiù zài yóu jú duì miàn　yóu jú de zuǒ bian shì zhěn
不远。超级市场就在邮局对面。邮局的左边是诊

suǒ　yòu bian shì yín háng　shì zhèng dà lóu zài bǎi huò gōng sī de qián mian
所，右边是银行。市政大楼在百货公司的前面。

wǒ jiā fù jìn hái yǒu yí ge dà jiào táng　jiào táng de hòu mian shì yí ge xiǎo
我家附近还有一个大教堂。教堂的后面是一个小

xué　páng biān shì yí ge gōng yuán
学，旁边是一个公园。

NEW WORDS

1. 市中心 (shì zhōng xīn) city centre
2. 生活 (shēng huó) life
3. 便 (biàn) convenient
   方便 (fāng biàn) convenient
4. 邮(郵) (yóu) post; mail
5. 局 (jú) bureau
   邮局 (yóu jú) post office
*6. 面 (miàn) side; aspect

7. 诊(診) (zhěn) examine (a patient)
   诊所 (zhěn suǒ) clinic
8. 银(銀) (yín) silver
   银行 (yín háng) bank
9. 贷(貨) (huò) goods
   百货公司 (bǎi huò gōng sī) department store
10. 政 (zhèng) administrative affairs of certain government departments

11. 市政 (shì zhèng) municipal administration
11. 教堂 (jiào táng) church
12. 前面 (qián mian) front
13. 后面 (hòu mian) back
14. 公园 (gōng yuán) park

1 Say the following in Chinese.

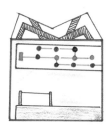
Example

地铁站

 1

 2

 3

 4

 5

 6

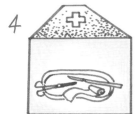 7

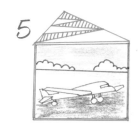 8

 9

 10

 11

 12

 13

 14

2 Interview your partner.

《Sample questions:

1	你们学校离你家远吗？你每天怎么上学？
2	你家离市中心远吗？你怎么去市中心？
3	你家住的地方生活方便吗？附近有什么商店？
4	你家附近有公共游泳池吗？你经常去那里游泳吗？
5	你家附近有公园吗？你经常去那里玩儿吗？
6	你家附近有公共图书馆吗？你经常去那里借书吗？
7	你家附近有教堂吗？你星期天通常去教堂吗？

Report to the class:

他们学校离他家不远。他每天走路上学。他家 ......

3 Activity.

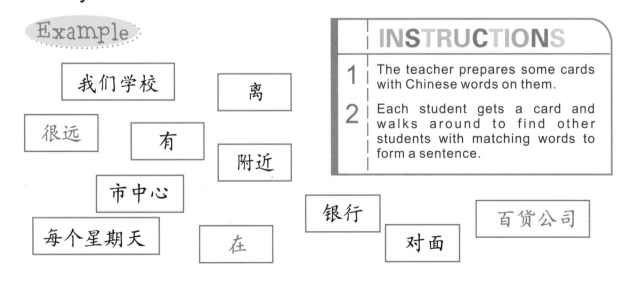

Example

我们学校	离
很远	有
	附近
市中心
每个星期天	在
银行	对面	百货公司

INSTRUCTIONS

1 The teacher prepares some cards with Chinese words on them.

2 Each student gets a card and walks around to find other students with matching words to form a sentence.

4 Complete the dialogue with your partner.

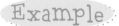Example

A: 医院在哪儿?

B: 在我家后面。

A: 公共图书馆在哪儿?

B: ......

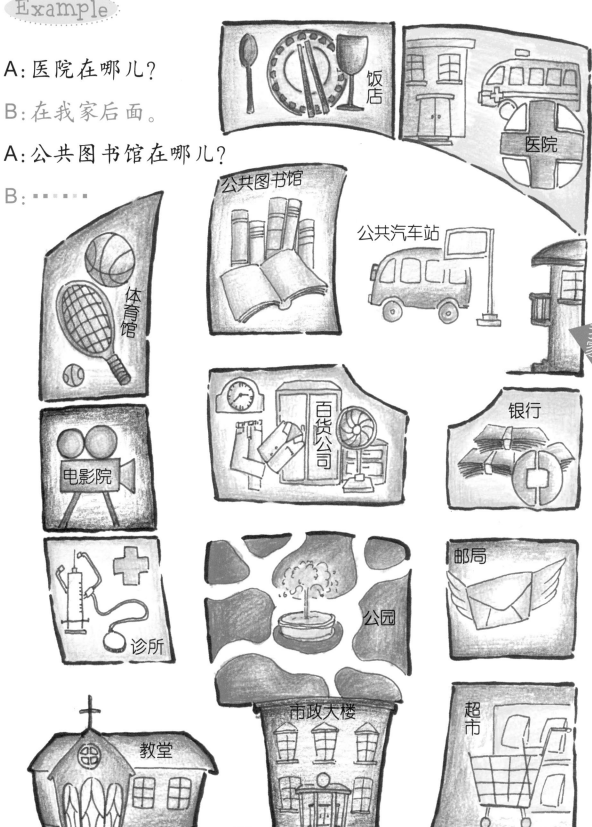

饭店

医院

公共图书馆

公共汽车站

我家

体育馆

银行

电影院

百货公司

诊所

公园

邮局

教堂

市政大楼

超市

125

5 Listen and put the right letter in the box.

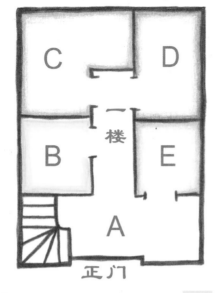
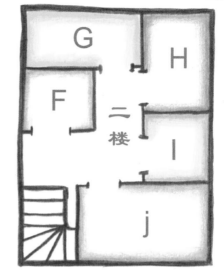

1. 哥哥的卧室 ☐   2. 客厅 ☐   3. 浴室 ☐

4. 爸爸、妈妈的卧室 ☐   5. 厨房 ☐   6. 书房 ☐

7. 小明的卧室 ☐   8. 电视房 ☐

6 Speaking practice.

Example

我家住的地方生活很方便。超市就在我家后门。我的学校就在附近，走路两分钟就到了。我家旁边有各种各样的商店，有······ 我家离市中心不远，坐车十分钟就到了。地铁站和公共汽车站······

It is your turn!

Draw a map of your neighbourhood and describe it.

126

①

qǐng wèn　　 kā fēi guǎn zài　 nǎr
A：请问，咖啡馆在哪儿？

nǐ xiān guò mǎ lù　　 rán hòu yì
B：你先过马路，然后一

zhí wǎng qián zǒu　　 zǒu wǔ fēn zhōng
直往前走，走五分钟

jiù dào le
就到了。

②

qǐng wèn　　 qù yín háng zěn me zǒu
A：请问，去银行怎么走？

nǐ yì zhí wǎng qián zǒu　　 kàn dào
B：你一直往前走，看到

hóng lǜ dēng xiàng zuǒ guǎi　　 zài zǒu
红绿灯向左拐，再走

wǔ fēn zhōng jiù dào le
五分钟就到了。

③

qǐng wèn　　 fù jìn yǒu yī yuàn ma
A：请问，附近有医院吗？

nǐ zài qián bian de dì yī ge lù
B：你在前边的第一个路

kǒu guò mǎ lù　　 rán hòu wǎng yòu
口过马路，然后往右

zhuǎn　　 yī yuàn jiù zài nǐ de yòu
转。医院就在你的右

shǒu biān
手边。

NEW WORDS

1. kā fēi 咖啡 coffee
   kā fēi guǎn 咖啡馆 café

*2. guò 过(過) cross

3. yì zhí 一直 straight

4. wǎng 往 towards
   wǎng qián 往前 forward

5. zhōng 钟(鐘) clock

6. kàn dào 看到 see

7. dēng 灯(燈) lamp
   hóng lù dēng 红绿灯 traffic lights

8. xiàng 向 towards

9. guǎi 拐 turn

10. dì 第 indicating ordinal numbers

11. lù kǒu 路口 intersection

12. zhuǎn 转(轉) turn

13. yòu shǒu 右手 right hand

7 Match the picture with the answer.

1
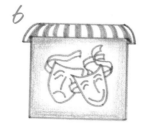

2

3

4

5

6

7

8

9

10

11

12

Answers

a) 中药房

b) 剧场

c) 灯具店

d) 五金店

e) 礼品店

f) 糕饼店

g) 理发店

h) 电器店

i) 茶馆

j) 钟表店

k) 便利店

l) 西洋乐器店

8 Match the picture with the answer.

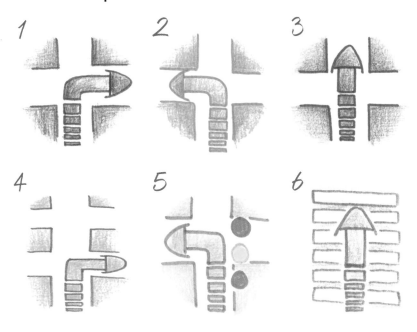

1   2   3

4   5   6

Answers

a) 往右拐

b) 向左转

c) 一直往前走

d) 过马路

e) 在第一个路口往右拐

f) 看见红绿灯往左拐

9 Make dialogues with your partner.

Example

A: 请问，去邮局怎么走?

B: ......

Sentences for Reference

a) 请问,去银行怎么走?

b) 你先过马路,然后一直往前走。

c) 走五分钟就到了。

d) 看到红绿灯过马路,再一直往前走。

e) 你在第二个路口往左拐。

f) 诊所就在你的右手边。

Situations

1. 去邮局   2. 去教堂

3. 去市政大楼

10 Activity.

邮局　银行　飞机场　百货公司

教堂　公园　律师　市政大楼

饭店　茶馆　菜市场

文具店

诊所　医院　电影院　咖啡馆

INSTRUCTIONS

1	The class is divided into two teams.
2	The team members line up on both sides of the classroom. One member from each team stands near the board.
3	The teacher puts up 10-15 cards with characters on the board. The teacher says one word, and the student who is the first to touch the card wins a point. The team which wins more points wins.

11 Make dialogues with your partner.

公共图书馆　医院　市政大楼　教堂　超市　公园　体育中心　咖啡馆　诊所　邮局　银行　百货公司　你

Example

A: 去教堂怎么走?

B: 在第一个路口往左拐。看见红绿灯向右拐。一直走,在第二个路口过马路,你就可以看到教堂了。

Situations

1. 去医院
2. 去体育中心
3. 去咖啡馆
4. 去市政大楼

130

12 Listen and write down the right letters.

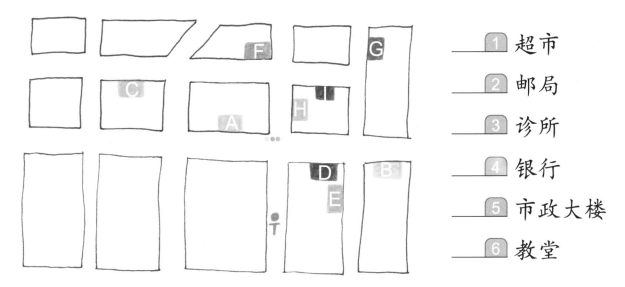

_____ 1 超市

_____ 2 邮局

_____ 3 诊所

_____ 4 银行

_____ 5 市政大楼

_____ 6 教堂

13 Speaking practice.

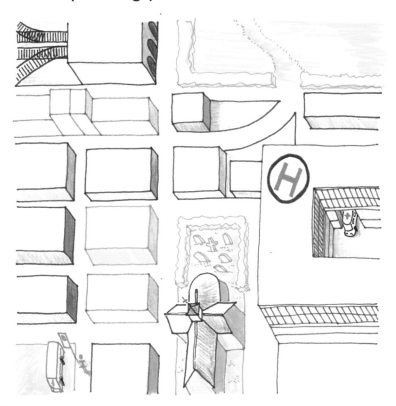

Example

如果从你家去市中心公园，你可以坐公共汽车去，或者走路去。你先过马路，然后一直走，在第三个路口向右拐，再一直往前走五分钟。你就可以看到市中心公园了。

It is your turn!

Look at the city map chosen and explain to your partner how to get to five places.

Lesson 14　Asking the Way　问路

Text 1　53

qǐng wèn　　qù bā fāng gòu wù guǎng chǎng zěn me zǒu
请问，去八方购物广场怎么走？

nǐ huò zhě qí zì xíng chē qù　　huò zhě zuò gōng gòng qì chē qù
你或者骑自行车去，或者坐公共汽车去。

zuò jǐ lù gōng gòng qì chē
坐几路公共汽车？

zuò　　lù huò　　lù dōu kě yǐ
坐25路或97路都可以。

chē zhàn zài　　nǎr
车站在哪儿？

jiù zài qián mian nà zuò miào de duì miàn
就在前面那座庙的对面。

wǒ yào zuò jǐ zhàn
我要坐几站？

dà gài zuò wǔ liù zhàn　　kàn jiàn yì
大概坐五六站。看见一
tiáo hé　　guò le dà qiáo yǐ hòu
条河，过了大桥以后，
zài gòu wù guǎng chǎng nà zhàn xià chē
在购物广场那站下车。

NEW WORDS

1. <ruby>购<rt>gòu</rt></ruby>(購) buy
   <ruby>购物<rt>gòu wù</rt></ruby> shopping
2. <ruby>广<rt>guǎng</rt></ruby>(廣) wide
   <ruby>广场<rt>guǎng chǎng</rt></ruby> square

3. <ruby>骑<rt>qí</rt></ruby>(騎) ride
4. <ruby>自行车<rt>zì xíng chē</rt></ruby> bicycle
✱5. <ruby>路<rt>lù</rt></ruby> route
6. <ruby>车站<rt>chē zhàn</rt></ruby> station; stop

7. <ruby>座<rt>zuò</rt></ruby> measure word
8. <ruby>庙<rt>miào</rt></ruby>(廟) temple
9. <ruby>河<rt>hé</rt></ruby> river
10. <ruby>桥<rt>qiáo</rt></ruby>(橋) bridge

1 Say one sentence about each picture.

Example

公园附近有很多
人力车，坐一次
五块钱。

1

2

3

4

5

6

7

8

9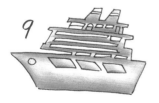

10

11

12

13

14

133

2 Complete the sentences.

1. 你或者走路去，<u>或者坐公共汽车去。</u>

2. 我们晚饭或者吃中餐，_____

3. 我明年或者学历史，_____

4. 今年暑假我或者 _____

5. 你感冒了。你或者吃中药，_____

6. 今天外面很冷。你或者穿_____

It is your turn!

Make two sentences with "或者".

3 Match the picture with the answer.

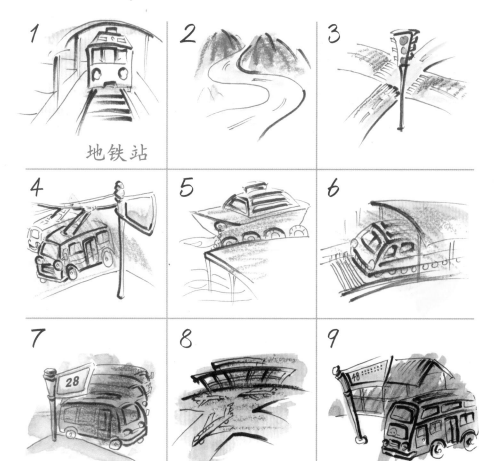

1. 地铁站

Answers

a) 公路
b) 小巴站
c) 码头
d) 马路
e) 电车站
f) 地铁站
g) 火车站
h) 机场
i) 公共汽车站

4 Make dialogues with your classmates.

Example

A:请问，去市政大楼怎么走？

B:你或者坐车去，或者走路去。

A:坐几路车？

B:五路或十八路都可以。

A:如果我想走路去，我该怎么走？

B:······

Sentences for Reference

a) 你或者坐车去，或者走路去。

b) 坐几路公共汽车？

c) 要坐几站？

d) 车站在哪儿？

e) 在哪站下车？

f) 看见公园就在下一站下车。

g) 在市政大楼那站下车。

飞机场

咖啡馆

购物广场

市政大楼

电影院

体育中心

公共图书馆

Situations

1. 去购物广场

2. 去飞机场

3. 去公共图书馆

4. 去电影院

5 Ask your classmates the following questions.

1. 从你家去学校，走路要多长时间？

2. 从你家去附近的商场，需要坐车吗？
   如果开车去，路上要多长时间？

3. 从你家去电影院怎么走？

4. 如果你坐飞机去北京，要飞几个小时？

5. 如果你去上海，可以坐船去吗？

6. 如果你去纽约，坐飞机大概要多长时间？

6 Listen and tick the right answers.

54

1 a) 她家附近没有电影院。 b) 她家附近没有汽车站。	**4** a) 菜市场里的东西便宜。 b) 她觉得超市里的东西便宜。
2 a) 家具店离她家不远。 b) 她家离鞋店特别远。	**5** a) 她家附近没有诊所。 b) 附近的诊所不小。
3 a) 他们家不常去超市买东西。 b) 超市就在她家楼下。	**6** a) 爸爸工作，妈妈不工作。 b) 爸爸的公司离她家不远。

小青 | 我在购物广场买东西的时候手提包被偷了。

警察 | 在哪家商店被偷的？

小青 | 在四彩服装店。

警察 | 包里有什么？

小青 | 有钱包、钥匙和手机。

警察 | 钱包里有什么？

小青 | 有两百多块现金、身份证、学生证和借书证。

警察 | 请留下你的姓名和电话号码。

小青 | 好。

137

NEW WORDS

shǒu tí bāo
1. 手提包 handbag

bèi
2. 被 a preposition

tōu
3. 偷 steal

jǐng
4. 警 short for police

chá
5. 察 examine

jǐng chá
警察 policeman

fú zhuāng
6. 服装 clothing

qián bāo
7. 钱包 wallet; purse

yào shi
8. 钥(鑰)匙 key

shǒu jī
9. 手机 mobile phone

xiàn jīn
10. 现金 cash

shēn
11. 身 body

fèn
12. 份 portion; measure word

shēn fèn
身份 identity

zhèng
13. 证(證) certificate; card

shēn fèn zhèng
身份证 identity card

xué shēng zhèng
学生证 student card

jiè shū zhèng
借书证 library card

liú
14. 留 leave

xìng
15. 姓 surname

xìng míng
姓名 full name

7 Make dialogues with your partner.

Example

A: 书包里有什么?

B: 有钱包、钥匙、文具盒、课本等。

A: 钱包里有什么?

B: 有现金、身份证、学生证和借书证。

A: 文具盒里有什么?

B: 有铅笔······

Situations

1.你们的汉语教室	2.你们学校	3.你们学校的图书馆
4.你家的客厅	5.你的房间	6.你家的厨房

8 Complete the sentences.

1. 我已经做完 作业了。
2. 弟弟吃完了 _____
3. 爸爸找到了 _____
4. 外面很冷，快穿上 ____

5. 他借走了我的 _____
6. 哥哥开走了爷爷的 ____
7. 姐姐花完了 _____
8. 妈妈听见了 _____

It is your turn!

Make two sentences with the structure of "complement of result".

9 Complete the sentences.

1. 我的三明治 被 狗 吃了。

2. _____ 被 小猫 _____

3. _____ 被 妈妈 开走了。

4. _____ 被 姐姐 借走了。

5. _____ 被 人 偷走了。

6. _____ 被 我的朋友 花光了。

7. _____ 被 我 吃光了。

NOTE

被 is used to indicate passive voice, e.g.

我的钱包被人偷了。

It is your turn!

Make two sentences with the "被" structure.

139

10 Make dialogues with your partner.

小亮：我的手机不见了。

服务员：什么时候不见的？在哪儿不见的？

小亮：五分钟前我还看见手机在桌上。

服务员：你的手机是什么颜色的？

小亮：黑色的。

服务员：请留下你的姓名和电话号码。我们找到你的手机后会打电话给你。

Situations

1. You have lost your wallet.
2. You have lost your school bag.

11 Listen and tick the right answers.

1
a) 手机被偷了。
b) 手机卖了。
c) 手机被借走了。

2
a) 上体育课
b) 上音乐课
c) 上美术课

3
a) 手机放在书包里。
b) 手机放在教室里。
c) 手机放在办公室里。

4
a) 去体育馆找过了
b) 去校长室找过了
c) 去教室找过了

5
a) 打电话给妈妈了
b) 去学校办公室问了
c) 问过朋友了

6
a) 他会再去教室找找。
b) 他回家再找找。
c) 他会去校长室找。

12 Ask your classmates the following questions.

1. 你家附近有购物商场吗？

2. 你常去哪儿购物？你一般去买什么东西？

3. 你最喜欢哪家商店？为什么？

4. 你最近有没有去买东西？去了哪家商店？买了什么？
   一共花了多少钱？

5. 你下个周末会去购物吗？你会跟谁一起去买东西？
   你想买什么？大概花多少钱？

13 Project.

INSTRUCTION

Suppose that you have one month's holiday, and you are going to travel around the world. Search for information you need on the internet and then present your travel route to the class.

Example

如果我有一个月的假期，我会去四个国家。我先从香港坐飞机去东京，大概要飞五个小时。我会在东京玩儿一个星期。从东京我会坐飞机去伦敦，路上大约要十一个半小时。我会在伦敦玩儿十天。从伦敦我会坐火车去巴黎，路上要三四个小时。我会在巴黎玩儿一个星期。从巴黎我会坐飞机去纽约，路上大约要七个半小时。我会在纽约玩儿大约五六天。

Text 1 57

wǒ men jiā zuì jìn
我们家最近
bān jiā le   xīn fán zi
搬家了。新房子
hěn hǎo   kě shì lóu shàng
很好，可是楼上
de lín jū hěn fán rén
的邻居很烦人。
wǒ zǎo shang wǔ diǎn jiù tīng
我早上五点就听
jiàn yǒu rén zài fáng jiān li
见有人在房间里
pǎo bù   wǎn shang shí èr
跑步。晚上十二
diǎn   tā men de diàn shì
点，他们的电视
jī hái kāi de hěn xiǎng
机还开得很响。
měi tiān bàn yè hái tīng jiàn
每天半夜还听见
hái zi kū
孩子哭。

NEW WORDS

zuì jìn
1. 最近 recently

bān
2. 搬 move

bān jiā
搬家 move (house)

lín
3. 邻(鄰) neighbour

jū
4. 居 live

lín jū
邻居 neighbour

fán
5. 烦(煩) annoy

fán rén
烦人 annoying

tīng jiàn
6. 听见 hear

xiǎng
7. 响(響) loud; noisy

yè
8. 夜 night

bàn yè
半夜 midnight

kū
9. 哭 cry

1 Describe the picture.

这是一幢三层楼的洋房。这幢洋房

有一个客厅 ▪▪▪▪▪▪

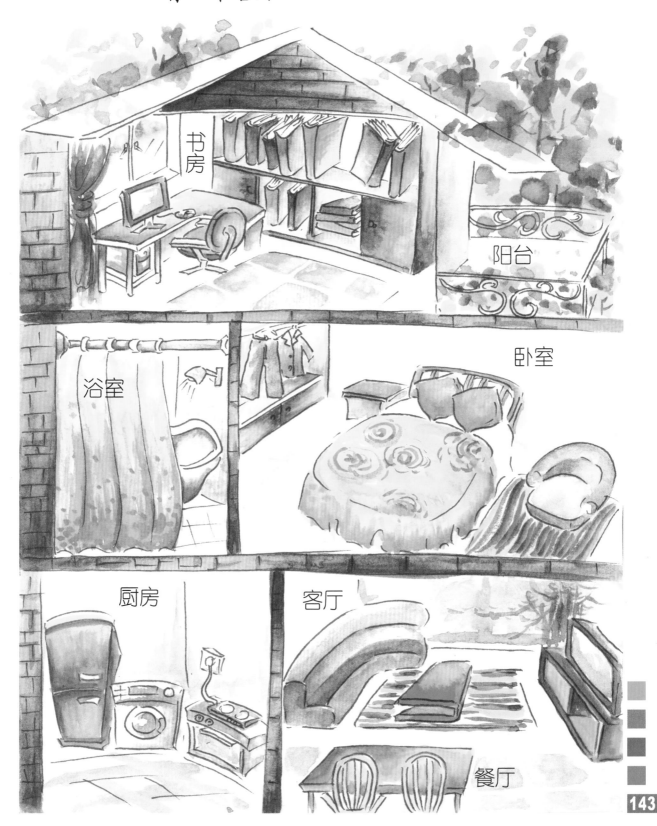

2 Activity.

1 昨天　今天　明天　后天

2 去年　今年　明年　后年

3 一天　半天　一天半

4 一年　半年　一年半

5 上个月　这个月　下个月

6 上个星期　这个星期　下个星期

7 一个月　半个月　一个半月

8 一个星期　半个星期　一个半星期

9 一个小时　半个小时　一个半小时

10 上午九点　下午三点　晚上八点　半夜两点

INSTRUCTIONS

1 The class is divided into pairs.

2 The teacher says a phrase in English and each pair is expected to write down the phrase in Chinese.

3 The pair writing more correct phrases than any other pair wins the activity.

It is your turn!

Choose five phrases on the left and make a sentence with each of them.

3 Ask your partner the following questions.

1 你最近有没有买新衣服？买了什么衣服？花了多少钱？

2 你们家最近有没有去饭店吃饭？去了哪家饭店？吃了什么？花了多少钱？

3 你们最近有没有考试？考了什么？考试难不难？你考得怎么样？

4 你们家最近几年有没有搬家？你们家现在住什么样的房子？你喜欢现在住的地方吗？

4 Say a few sentences about each picture.

我跑步跑(得)很快。我
很喜欢跑步，我每天
早上跑一个小时。

Words for Reference

a) 可是／但是

b) 因为

c) 所以

d) 特别喜欢

e) 非常不喜欢

f) 最喜欢

g) 平时

h) 通常

i) 经常／常常

j) 很会

1

2

3

4

5

6

7

5 Listen and tick the right answers.

1 a)楼上邻居养猫。 b)楼下邻居有小孩儿。 c)楼上邻居养狗。	*4* a)邻居养了猫。 b)邻居养了狗。 c)邻居养了鸟。
2 a)在家玩儿电脑游戏 b)在家踢球 c)在家唱歌	*5* 邻居_____。 a)每天晚上看电影 b)每个周末在家看电影 c)家里每天晚上有小孩儿叫
3 a)电视机开得响。 b)音乐开得响。 c)有人在跑步。	*6* 邻居晚上在房间里_____。 a)跑步 b)跳舞 c)打字

6 Make a sentence with each of the dotted words.

1. 今天很冷，你要⟨多⟩穿点儿衣服。

2. 不要在这儿过马路。你应该在红绿灯那儿过。

3. 去商场不用坐车，走路五分钟就到了。

4. 因为今天有大风雪，所以学校都关门。

5. 如果你暑假去北京，你应该带汗衫和短裤。

6. 这双靴子太贵了，我不买了。

7. 我每天一起床就洗澡，然后吃早饭。

8. 昨天我的钱包被人偷了。

9. 我从小就喜欢吃中餐。

10. 上课的时候不可以说话。

^{wǒ jiù zhù zài lóu xià} ^{měi tiān zǎo shang}
我就住在楼下。每天早上
^{yǒu rén zài fáng jiān li pǎo bù} ^{duì ma}
有人在房间里跑步，对吗？

^{duì}
对。

^{nǐ bǎ wǒ chǎo xǐng le}
你把我吵醒了。

^{duì bu qǐ} ^{wǒ yǐ hòu wǎn yì diǎnr pǎo}
对不起。我以后晚一点儿跑。

^{měi tiān wǎn shang} ^{nǐ men de diàn shì jī kāi de}
每天晚上，你们的电视机开得
^{hěn xiǎng} ^{qǐng wèn néng bu néng xiǎo diǎnr shēng}
很响。请问能不能小点儿声？

^{hǎo} ^{wǒ yǐ hòu zhù yì}
好，我以后注意。

^{měi tiān bàn yè} ^{wǒ hái tīng jiàn xiǎo hái zi kū}
每天半夜，我还听见小孩子哭。

^{duì bu qǐ} ^{xiǎo hái zi kū} ^{wǒ méi yǒu bàn fǎ}
对不起，小孩子哭，我没有办法。

NEW WORDS

* 1. 把 bǎ a preposition
2. 吵 chǎo make a noise; quarrel
3. 醒 xǐng wake up

4. 声(聲) shēng sound
5. 注 zhù concentrate
注意 zhù yì pay attention to

6. 法 fǎ method; way
办法 bàn fǎ way

7 Rewrite the following sentences with the "把" structure.

1. 他吃完了两个苹果。→ 他把两个苹果吃完了。

2. 请关上电视机。_____

3. 请给我你的练习本。_____

4. 请写下你的姓名。_____

5. 叔叔骑走了爸爸的车。_____

6. 谁偷走了我的钱包？_____

7. 妈妈早上叫醒了我。_____

NOTE

The 把 structure emphasizes the receiver of the action, e.g.

弟弟喝了牛奶。
→弟弟把牛奶喝了。

8 Activity.

1. 开车   2. 唱歌   3. 穿衣服

4. 跳高   5. 咳嗽   6. 说汉语

7. 吃饭   8. 喝水   9. 量体温

10. 看书   11. 坐车   12. 搬桌子

13. 钓鱼   14. 滑雪   15. 戴帽子

16. 打篮球 17. 踢足球 18. 打排球

INSTRUCTIONS

1 The whole class may join the activity.

2 When the teacher says an action word, the students are expected to act accordingly.

3 Those who act wrongly are out of the activity.

148

9 Describe the picture.

Example 他们正在干什么呢？

他们正在吵架。

10 Complete the sentences.

1. _____请跑得_____ 快一点儿。
2. _____ 大一点儿。
3. _____ 高一点儿。
4. _____ 远一点儿。
5. _____ 响一点儿。

6. _____ 好一点儿。
7. _____ 圆一点儿。
8. _____ 直一点儿。
9. _____ 多一点儿。
10. _____ 低一点儿。

11 Role play.

Example

A: 我正在做作业。能不能
　　小点儿声说话?

B: 对不起。

Situations

1. 音乐开得很响。

2. 半夜有人在房间里唱歌。

3. 小孩儿在房间里踢球。

4. 两个男孩儿在楼上打乒乓球。

12 Complete the following dialogues.

请注意,车来了。

谢谢你提醒我。

我有很多笔。这支笔借给你用吧。

Sentences for Reference

a) 谢谢你。

b) 非常感谢!

c) 不用客气。

d) 没关系。

e) 对不起。

f) 请注意。

g) 谢谢你提醒我。

1　2
3　4

谢谢你帮我提箱子。

对不起。以后我小声点儿。

It is your turn!

Create four situations and make dialogues with your partner.

150

13 Listen and tick the right answers.

1 王先生的	a)女儿跳舞	b)儿子踢球	c)小狗天天叫
2 周太太家	a)有人唱歌	b)电视机开得响	c)音乐开得太响
3 王小姐	a)养猫	b)养狗	c)养鸟
4 小英	a)在玩儿电脑	b)在听音乐	c)在弹钢琴
5 小天	a)在打篮球	b)在踢球	c)在看电视
6 小明	a)爱看电视	b)爱做作业	c)爱唱歌

14 Role play.

Example

A: 借我一支铅笔用一下，行吗?

B: 你已经借去五支铅笔了。还没有还给我呢。

A: 是吗? 对不起，我忘了。

B: 今天再借给你一支。用完请还给我。

A: 好的,谢谢。

Sentences for Reference

a) 这是最后一次, 下次不借了。

b) 你是天下大好人。

c) 我知道你心肠好。

d) 我知道你会帮我。

e) 借我一支笔,可以吗?

f) 对不起,我忘了还给你。

g) 用完请还给我。

Situations

1. 每天跟你借橡皮。

2. 经常跟你借钱，有时候不还。

3. 每天晚上十点以后打电话给你。

4. 每天不带午饭，想吃你的午饭。

15 Describe the picture.

Example

我家住在一幢三层楼的楼房里。一共有九户人家住在这幢楼里。我们家住三楼，301室。王伯伯住在隔壁。他是一个很烦人的邻居。半夜一点，他的电视机还开得很响••••••

It is your turn!

Describe your neighbours.

要买的东西

- 床
-
-
-
-
-
-
-

INSTRUCTION

- This can be a joint project managed by two students.
- Each team is expected to draw the layout of a house on an A4 size paper, and write up a list of things to furnish the house on a separate piece of paper.
- The class together with the teacher judge each project based on the design, the quality of drawing and the language used.

Listening Scripts 听力录音稿

Unit 1 Lesson 1

P4

1) 小明一家住在伦敦。爸爸、妈妈都在伦敦工作。
2) 小明有两个伯伯。大伯住在纽约，二伯住在洛杉矶。
3) 小明的爷爷、奶奶住在上海。他们也去过美国。
4) 小明的姑姑在北京工作。
5) 小明的叔叔在香港上大学。

P9

1) 小天的爷爷去年去世了。
2) 我姨妈家有一个儿子、两个女儿。
3) 我们每年跟爷爷、奶奶一起过春节。
4) 小明家的亲戚都住在中国。
5) 我外公、外婆跟姨妈住在上海。
6) 我们常常跟大伯一家见面。

Unit 1 Lesson 2

P13

1) 她有点儿胖。她大眼睛、大嘴巴。她的头发长长的。
2) 她很瘦。她小眼睛、大耳朵。她的头发是黑色的。
3) 他长得又高又瘦，腿长长的。
4) 他长得矮矮的，头发是黄色的，很短。他有高高的鼻子。

P18

1) A: 你昨天晚上是什么时候睡觉的?
   B: 十点半左右。
2) A: 你奶奶长什么样?
   B: 她的个子矮矮的，有一米五左右。她穿黑衣服。
3) A: 你每天上学穿什么样的校服?
   B: 我穿白色的衬衫和蓝色的短裙。
4) A: 你们每年在哪儿过圣诞节?
   B: 在上海的外公、外婆家。
5) A: 你有爷爷、奶奶吗?
   B: 有爷爷，奶奶去年去世了。
6) A: 你家亲戚多吗?
   B: 不太多。我有一个叔叔、一个姑姑,还有两个舅舅和一个姨妈。

Unit 1 Lesson 3

P24

1) A: 你哪儿不舒服?
   B: 我又头痛又咳嗽。我还发烧。
2) A: 你是从什么时候开始发烧的?
   B: 从昨天晚上。
3) A: 我们要去外婆家吗?
   B: 对。你外公生病了。他又发烧又咳嗽。
4) A: 小英今天来上学了吗?
   B: 她没来。她妈妈打电话来,说她生病了。
5) A: 你两天没来上学。你去哪儿了?
   B: 我感冒了。医生叫我在家休息两天。

6) A：我嗓子疼，不能说话。
   B：我给你开一点儿药。你要多喝水，少说话。

P28 12

1) A：你哪儿不舒服？
   B：我的脚受伤了，很痛。
2) A：你的腿是什么时候受伤的？
   B：我上午上体育课的时候受伤的。
3) A：你昨天去哪儿了？
   B：我妈妈带我去看医生了。
4) A：我明天能上学吗？
   B：不可以，你需要在家休息两天。
5) A：我需要吃药吗？
   B：不用。你要多休息，多喝水。
6) A：你发烧了，三十九度四。
   B：所以说我觉得不舒服。

Unit 2 Lesson 4

P33 14

1) A：北京的春天天气怎么样？
   B：挺冷的。常常刮风，不常下雨。
2) A：香港夏天常刮台风吗？
   B：有时候刮。
3) A：伦敦的冬天下雪吗？
   B：有时候下雪。下雪的时候要穿大衣。
4) A：今天的天气太好了！我们去游泳吧。
   B：好。我们四点在游泳池见。
5) A：我们几点去看电影？
   B：下午三点半，好吗？
6) A：你的腿怎么了？
   B：我跑步的时候受伤了。

P39 16

1) A：你今年暑假会去哪儿？
   B：会去日本，因为我们要去看爷爷、奶奶。
2) A：你去年寒假去哪儿了？
   B：去法国看姑姑了。姑姑一家住在法国。
3) A：夏天去上海要穿什么衣服？
   B：要穿汗衫和短裤。上海夏天很热。
4) A：冬天去北京应该带什么衣服？
   B：要带大衣、毛衣、长裤，还要带帽子、围巾和手套。
5) A：你出去最好带一把雨伞。今天有雨。
   B：不用带雨伞。我会带雨衣。
6) A：因为今天下大雨，所以体育课不游泳了。
   B：我们打篮球吧。

Unit 2 Lesson 5

P43 18

1) A：你爸爸做什么工作？
   B：他是工程师，在一家英国公司工作。
2) A：你爸爸每天穿什么衣服上班？
   B：他穿衬衫和长裤，有时候穿西装。
3) A：你爸爸工作忙不忙？
   B：特别忙，每天很晚回家，常常出差。
4) A：你妈妈做什么工作？
   B：她是秘书，在一所学校工作。
5) A：你妈妈上班喜欢穿什么衣服？
   B：她喜欢穿衬衫和裙子，有时候穿套装。

6) A：你每天上学穿校服吗？

B：穿。我穿白色的衬衫和棕色的长裤。

P49

1) A：这个三人沙发多少钱？

B：五千七百三十八块。

2) A：这条连衣裙多少钱？有红色的吗？

B：七百九十九块。有红色、蓝色和紫色的。

3) A：这套餐桌、椅多少钱？

B：餐桌六千五百块，一把椅子七百块。

4) A：我想买西装，有四十号的吗？

B：有。你最好穿三十八号的。

5) A：这双皮鞋多少钱？有白色的吗？

B：五百八十块。除了黑色的，还有白色和棕色的。

6) A：我可以试试这条领带吗？

B：对不起，领带不可以试。

Unit 2 Lesson 6

P54

1) 我小时候住在北京。我九岁跟爸爸、妈妈去了美国。

2) 我们一家人喜欢滑雪，每年冬天都会去加拿大滑雪。

3) 除了羽毛球以外，我每个星期还会跟爸爸打乒乓球。

4) 我小时候住在英国。周末常常跟爸爸一起去钓鱼。

5) 我昨天去滑冰了。我跟朋友一起去的。

6) 今天很冷，零下十度。现在正在下雪。

P57

1) A：这件游泳衣多少钱？有大号的吗？

B：对不起，没有大号的了，有中号和小号的。

2) A：我可以试一下这顶帽子吗？

B：当然可以。

3) A：这副耳环多少钱？我可以试试吗？

B：对不起，耳环不可以试。

4) A：这种运动裤有蓝色的吗？

B：有。请等一等，我去帮你拿。

5) A：这条项链多少钱？我可以看一下吗？

B：当然可以。你要不要试一试？

6) A：这种手套有几种颜色？

B：有白色和黑色的。

Unit 3 Lesson 7

P64

1) 小东最喜欢数学，因为他的数学老师对他很好。

2) 小明特别喜欢学化学，因为他觉得化学很有趣。

3) 小文挺喜欢学生物的，但是她觉得生物难学。

4) 大生喜欢学语言，英语、汉语，他都喜欢。他觉得英语和汉语都很有用。

5) 小天不喜欢唱歌，也不喜欢跳舞。他对音乐不感兴趣。

6) 小雪非常爱读历史书。她对历史特别感兴趣。

1) A：你今年学几门课？学什么课？
   B：我学十三门课。我学数学、英语、汉语、科学、电脑、戏剧、体育等。
2) A：你最喜欢哪门课？
   B：我最喜欢科学，因为我对科学非常感兴趣。
3) A：你从什么时候开始学汉语的？
   B：我从小学三年级开始学的。
4) A：你为什么学汉语？
   B：因为我喜欢学语言。我觉得汉语很有用。
5) A：你不喜欢学哪门课？为什么？
   B：我不喜欢学物理，因为老师教得不好。
6) A：你每天功课多吗？要做多长时间？
   B：我每天的功课不太多，要做一个半小时。

Unit 3 Lesson 8

1) 我们学校挺大的，有六幢教学楼，每幢楼有六层。
2) 我周末常常去公共图书馆看书或者做功课。图书馆有十层。
3) 学校的礼堂不太大，但是有两层。
4) 在学校，我中午休息的时候常常跟朋友一起打篮球。
5) 我们学校的足球场非常大。我每天下午踢足球。
6) 学校离我家不远，走路十分钟就到了。

1) A：图书馆在哪儿？
   B：在六号教学楼。在二层。
2) A：化学实验室在哪儿？
   B：在物理实验室隔壁，在二楼。
3) A：附近有厕所吗？
   B：有，超市的二层有厕所。
4) A：教师办公室在哪儿？
   B：在校长办公室和图书馆的中间。
5) A：英文小说在几层？
   B：在四层。
6) A：美术室在一楼吗？
   B：不，在二楼，在电脑室的隔壁。

Unit 3 Lesson 9

1) 小明今天有数学课，可是他没有带尺子。
2) 小文今天没有带文具盒，也没有带课本。
3) 小东的文具盒里有橡皮和铅笔。
4) 大生买了一本日记本，花了二十五块。
5) 小天没有卷笔刀，妈妈给他买了两个。
6) 小花没有钢笔，她从学校的文具店里买了一支，花了三十五块。

1) A：你的日记本呢？
   B：我忘记带了。今天是第一次忘记带日记本。

2) A：借我汉语课本用一下，好吗？我忘记带了。

B：在这里。

3) A：我忘记带计算器了，借我用一下，好吗？

B：对不起，我正用呢。

4) A：我忘记带文具盒了。借我一支铅笔，好吗？

B：下课别忘了还给我。

5) A：我忘记带钱包了，借我二十块钱，行吗？

B：对不起，我也没有钱了。

6) A：我今天忘记带运动鞋了，我穿皮鞋，行吗？

B：不行，去跟别的同学借一双。

Unit 4 Lesson 10

P94 38

1) 今天的鱼很新鲜。黄鱼每斤二十八块。

2) 这里的牛排是澳大利亚进口的，四十五块一斤。

3) 快来买鸡腿！美国进口的鸡腿，二十块一斤。

4) 本地的活虾，又大又新鲜，三十九块一斤。

5) 快来买豆腐！两块钱一块。

6) 今天的猪肉特别新鲜，快来买，二十四块一斤。

P97 40

A：你们学校有几家餐厅？

B：有一家。

A：餐厅卖些什么？

B：卖小吃、午饭、各种饮料、水果等。

A：有什么午饭？

B：有三明治、汉堡包、热狗、炸鸡翅，还有不同的盒饭。

A：盒饭贵不贵？多少钱一盒？

B：不算贵，十九块钱一盒。

A：你午饭一般吃什么？

B：我常常吃盒饭，有时候也吃三明治。

A：你在学校的时候喝什么？

B：我差不多每天都买饮料喝。我不爱喝水。

Unit 4 Lesson 11

P104 42

1) A：你喜欢吃零食吗？

B：非常喜欢。我差不多每天都在学校买零食。

2) A：你每天吃什么零食？

B：各种各样的。我一般吃糖果、饼干、薯片等。

3) A：你常常喝汽水吗？

B：每天都喝。我平时爱喝汽水，最爱喝可乐。

4) A：你知道糖果对牙齿不好吗？

B：知道。但我从小就喜欢吃糖，还爱吃巧克力。

5) A：你平时正餐吃得多不多？

B：我早饭吃得多，但是晚饭通常吃得少。

6) A：你每天去学校要带多少零用钱？

B：妈妈每天给我四十块。

P108

1) A：你今天早饭想吃什么？吃不吃面包、煎蛋？

B：我昨天就吃了面包、煎蛋。今天吃谷类早餐加牛奶吧。

2) A：你的茶里要不要加牛奶和糖？

B：加奶吧，不要加糖。

3) A：我们今天中午吃什么？吃汉堡包吧。

B：昨天吃了汉堡。今天吃炸鸡腿和沙拉吧。

4) A：你昨天晚饭吃了什么？

B：比萨饼和沙拉。我们去饭店吃的。

5) A：你们家平时吃中餐还是西餐？

B：差不多每天吃中餐，很少吃西餐。

6) A：你们家谁做饭？

B：平常是妈妈做，我有时候会帮妈妈做。吃过晚饭，我经常洗碗。

Unit 4 Lesson 12

P114

1) A：你们家周末常去饭店吃饭吗？

B：常去，大概每个星期一次。

2) A：你们常常去哪儿吃饭？

B：我们常去一家西式饭店吃自助餐。

3) A：你们上个周末去吃了吗？

B：没有，因为爸爸不舒服。我们在家吃的。

4) A：那家饭店什么菜做得最好吃？

B：他们的烤牛排做得非常好吃。我们每次都要吃。

5) A：去那家饭店吃饭的人多不多？

B：很多，因为他们的饭菜又好吃又便宜。

6) A：你们下个周末会去饭店吃饭吗？

B：不会去，因为爸爸出差了，下个月回来。

P119

1) 小天小时候不爱吃蔬菜，现在爱吃了。他每天晚饭都会吃蔬菜。

2) 小文爱吃水果。她最爱吃西瓜和梨。

3) 小山从小就爱吃快餐，每个周末都会吃汉堡包，所以现在很胖。

4) 冬冬最爱吃零食，每天在学校买零食吃。他爱吃薯片、巧克力、冰淇淋，还常常喝汽水。

5) 小云早上吃面包、煎蛋，喝一杯牛奶；中午在学校的餐厅里买盒饭吃。

6) 小明常和家人去北京饭店吃饭。他们爱吃北京烤鸭、红烧豆腐和炒肉丝。

Unit 5 Lesson 13

P126

1) 小明家住洋房，有两层。一进大门就是客厅。客厅的右边是厨房。

2) 小明和哥哥的卧室都在左手边，小明的卧室在厨房的对面。

3) 浴室就在哥哥的卧室对面。

4) 爸爸、妈妈的卧室在楼上，在右手边，一上楼就看见了。

5) 书房在爸爸、妈妈卧室的隔壁。

6) 电视房在右手边，在书房的隔壁。

P131

1) 去超市要先一直往前走，在第一个路口往右拐。大概要走两分钟。

2) 去邮局要一直往前走，看见红绿灯过马路。邮局在你的右手边。

3) 去诊所要先一直往前走，然后往右转两次。要走五分钟左右。

4) 去银行你要先往前走，在第二个路口过马路。过了马路你就看见银行了。

5) 去市政大楼要先往前走，在第一个路口往左拐，要走两分钟。市政大楼就在你的对面。

6) 去教堂要先一直往前走，在第二个路口往右拐，再走两分钟。过了马路你就可以看见教堂了。

Unit 5 Lesson 14

P136

1) A: 从你家怎么去电影院？
   B: 我一般坐公共汽车去。

2) A: 你家附近有什么商店？
   B: 有服装店、家具店、书店、鞋店等。

3) A: 你们家经常去哪儿买蔬菜、水果？
   B: 妈妈常去超市买，因为超市就在我们家楼下。

4) A: 超市里的东西贵不贵？
   B: 我觉得超市里的东西比菜市场里的贵一点儿。

5) A: 你生病去哪儿看医生？
   B: 离我家不远的地方有一家诊所，挺大的。

6) A: 你爸爸、妈妈工作的地方远吗？
   B: 爸爸就在附近的一个公司工作，妈妈的公司比较远。

P140

A: 我的手机被偷了。

B: 被偷了？是什么时候被偷的？

A: 上体育课的时候。我记得手机就放在书包里。

B: 你的书包放在哪儿了？

A: 就放在体育馆门口。

B: 你有没有去体育馆找一找？

A: 找过好几次了，但是没有找到。

B: 去学校办公室问过了吗？

A: 问过了，那里也没有。

B: 那你回家再找一找，有可能你忘记带去学校了。

A: 好吧，我今天回家再找一找。

Unit 5 Lesson 15

P146

1) 我家楼上的邻居最近养了一只狗，晚上总是听见狗叫，真烦人。

2) 我家隔壁的孩子每天晚上在家里踢球，真烦人。

3) 小明家的邻居每天晚上看电视。电视机开得很响，真烦人。

4) 小天的邻居养了一只鸟，每天早上五点就开始叫了，真烦人。

5) 小东的邻居每个周末都在家里看电影，声音很响，真烦人。

6) 小云家楼上的邻居每天晚上在家
里跳舞，音乐开得很响，真烦人。

P151  60

1) A: 王先生，你的女儿总是晚上在
      客厅里跳舞。能不能叫她不要
      在晚上跳。
   B: 对不起，我去跟她说。

2) A: 周太太，你们家的电视开得太
      响了。能不能小点儿声？
   B: 好，我们把声音开得小一点儿。

3) A: 王小姐，你们家的鸟总是早上
      叫，把我吵醒了。能不能把它
      放在别的地方？
   B: 对不起，我会把它放在别的房
      间里。

4) A: 小英，你的音乐开得太大声了，
      很吵。能不能开得小声点儿？
   B: 对不起，我现在就把声音开得
      小一点儿。

5) A: 小天，别在房间里踢球。你会
      把弟弟吵醒的。
   B: 好，我去外面踢。

6) A: 小明，你能不能把电视机关上？
      你看了一晚上电视了。
   B: 好，我不看了。